This You Can Believe

Faith Seeking Understanding

A Revised Edition With Study Guides

John R. Brokhoff

CSS Publishing Company, Inc., Lima, Ohio

THIS YOU CAN BELIEVE (REVISION)

Copyright © 1999 by
CSS Publishing Company, Inc.
Lima, Ohio

Some scripture quotations are from the *Revised Standard Version of the Bible*, copyrighted 1946, 1952 (c), 1971, 1973, by the Division of Christian Education of the National Council of the Churches of Christ in the USA. Used by permission.

Some scripture quotations are from the *New Revised Standard Version of the Bible*, copyright 1989 by the Division of Christian Education of the National Council of the Churches of Christ in the USA. Used by permission.

Library of Congress Cataloging-in-Publication Data

Brokhoff, John R.
    This you can believe : faith seeking understanding / John Brokhoff. — Rev. ed.
        p.   cm.
    ISBN 0-7880-1333-5 (pbk.)
    1. Apostles' Creed. I. Title.
BT993.2.B66   1999
238'.11—dc21   •   98-48040
                                        CIP

This book is available in the following formats, listed by ISBN:
    0-7880-1333-5   Book
    0-7880-1334-3   Disk
    0-7880-1335-1   Sermon Prep

PRINTED IN U.S.A.

*To all who are interested in
and concerned to mature
in their Christian faith.*

Table Of Contents

God The Holy Spirit

Foreword

An Adventure In Faith

With this book, *This You Can Believe*, we begin an exciting adventure in faith. It will be our map and motivation.

It is an adventure in gaining a greater faith. Because of shallow faith, every sincere Christian seeks a deeper faith. A recent periodical claims that one-third of Americans are ignorant of the Christian story. They have no framework and no knowledge of Christian theology or history.

In Jesus' day there was the same need for more faith. One time the disciples asked Jesus to "Increase our faith" (Luke 17:5). Just before leaving the Last Supper in the Upper Room for Gethsemane, Jesus said to Peter, "I have prayed for you that *your faith fail not*" (Luke 22:32). When Jesus came down from the Mount of Transfiguration, he healed an epileptic boy. His father said to Jesus, "If you can do anything, have pity on us and help us." Jesus replied, "All things are possible to him who believes." The father then cried, "I believe; help my unbelief" (Mark 9:24).

Yes, we have some faith. If we had no faith, we would not have bought this book or we would not be in a class using this book as a textbook. Americans do have some faith, according to a recent study:

- Nine in ten say they believe in God.
- Seven in ten believe in life after death.
- Eight in ten believe God works miracles.
- Nine in ten say they pray. (*Readers Digest*, May 1991, p. 84)

But it is not only a matter of having faith but of increasing our faith. We are therefore on an adventure of overcoming our unbelief.

Understanding Our Faith

We are on an adventure of not only increasing our faith but understanding our faith. Without a proper understanding, our faith may be useless. Which comes first: believing or understanding? Saint Augustine (354-430) had the answer: "Do not seek to understand in order to believe, but believe that you may understand."

Saint Anselm (1033-1109), archbishop of Canterbury, agreed when he said, "Faith seeks understanding." So in this book we will let our faith seek understanding of the truths in the Apostles' Creed.

Do we understand what we say we believe? Jesus faced this problem with his listeners. He asked the Pharisees, "Why do you not understand what I say?" (John 8:43). The disciples had the same problem. After his resurrection Jesus opened the minds of the apostles to understand the scriptures (Luke 24:45). When Philip encountered an Ethiopian eunuch reading Isaiah, he asked, "Do you understand what you are reading?" (Acts 8:30).

Understanding our faith can be a problem today. Do you understand the following:

- What is the meaning of faith?
- Does the evolution theory contradict the Genesis account of creation?
- What does it mean to be saved?
- Is the resurrection of Jesus physical fact or mental fiction?
- Is the Holy Spirit a "ghost" for you?

The Focus Of Our Adventure

The focus of our adventure is the Apostles' Creed. It is the church's statement of true Christian faith. Though it is called "Apostles' Creed," the apostles did not write it. It is anonymous. It is called "Apostles' Creed" because it expresses the faith of the apostles. In the first centuries of the church, the Apostles' Creed was known and used as "the rule of faith." If a person sincerely confessed this creed, the person was worthy to be baptized into the Christian faith. Therefore, this creed is central and basic to Christian faith.

Consider some of the characteristics of this creed:

1. **Ancient**. It is the oldest Christian creed dating from the first century. For twenty centuries millions upon millions of people based their faith on it. It expressed for them what a Christian believes.

2. **Apostolic**. The creed contains the faith of the apostles. Of all people, they knew Jesus best. For three years they lived day and night with him, saw his miracles, listened to his teachings, and witnessed his death and resurrection.

8

3. **Ecumenical.** The creed is accepted and used by all churches: Roman Catholic, Eastern Orthodox, and Protestant. No one church has a monopoly on it. Even if some Protestant churches do not use the creed in worship, they hold to the truths of the Creed.

4. **Brief.** In the traditional version of the Creed there are only 109 words. Each word is meaningful and essential, as our future study will show. In spite of its brevity, not one important teaching of the Bible is omitted.

5. **Simple.** The Creed is clear, simple, and easy to understand. For a contrast, examine the Athanasian Creed. The Apostles' Creed is easy for people of all ages to memorize.

6. **Theological.** The Holy Trinity is the main teaching of the Creed. It tells us the truth about God, Jesus, and the Holy Spirit. The work of the triune God is expressed in creation, redemption, and sanctification. All you need to know about God is in the Apostles' Creed. Thanks be to God for it!

Participation In The Adventure

Adventure calls for participation. We are the ones taking the adventure. We learn by listening and doing. Probably we learn more by doing the truth. To encourage your participation in the study of the Creed, a study guide is added after each chapter. It can be used for individual study. After each chapter, turn to the exercises in the study guide. If you are in a group study, the study guide will suggest topics for class discussion.

This You Can Believe can be used as a textbook for individual or group study in the church school as an elective for youth or adults. It is also a basic course for those interested in knowing the Christian faith before becoming members of a church.

This book is the product of sixty years of teaching in the faith of the church expressed by the Apostles' Creed. The course has been tested and tried, discussed and argued. For ten years the book has been used by hundreds of churches and thousands of believers seeking an understanding of their faith. Now it seems appropriate for the book to be revised and augmented. It is the hope and prayer of the author that this revised study will bring to you a greater faith and a deeper understanding of our precious faith.

The Apostles' Creed

Traditional Text

I believe in God the Father Almighty, maker of heaven and earth.

And in Jesus Christ, his only Son our Lord, who was conceived by the Holy Ghost, born of the Virgin Mary, suffered under Pontius Pilate, was crucified, dead, and buried. He descended into hell; the third day he rose again from the dead; he ascended into heaven, and sitteth on the right hand of God the Father Almighty; from thence he shall come to judge the quick and the dead.

I believe in the Holy Ghost; the holy catholic church, the communion of saints; the forgiveness of sins; the resurrection of the body, and the life everlasting. Amen.

Ecumenical Text

I believe in God, the Father almighty, creator of heaven and earth.

I believe in Jesus Christ, his only Son, our Lord. He was conceived by the power of the Holy Spirit and born of the virgin Mary. He suffered under Pontius Pilate, was crucified, died, and was buried. He descended to the dead. On the third day he rose again. He ascended into heaven, and is seated at the right hand of the Father. He will come again to judge the living and the dead.

I believe in the Holy Spirit, the holy catholic church, the communion of saints, the forgiveness of sins, the resurrection of the body, and the life everlasting. Amen.

Introduction

Chapter 1

Choose Your Belief

Today's Wilderness Of Beliefs

It is difficult to find Christian belief in today's world. Beliefs of all kinds abound.

First, there is the number of different churches. In the world it is reported that there are 23,500 denominations. In the United States there are 1,600. This leads to a diversity of convictions. This diversity was revealed in a poll of "born again" Christians.

- 32% agreed that "people's prayers do not have the power to change their circumstances."
- 49% agreed: "All good people, whether they consider Jesus Christ to be their Savior or not, will live in heaven after they die."
- 28% said this statement is true: "The whole idea of sin is outdated."

In addition, there is the current popularity of sects and cults. It is reported that there are 3,000 in America with three million adherents. One of these cults recently rented a house in San Diego in which forty adults committed suicide one night to release their souls from their bodies in order to meet a spaceship which supposedly was to take them to heaven.

For some people this results in confusion. For example, a man, feeling badly, went to church and responded to the altar call. When he knelt, a member of the church knelt beside him and said, "Hold on, brother, hold on. If you want to find God, hold on." A little later another member knelt beside him, put his arm around his shoulder and said, "Turn loose, brother. If you really want to know God, you have to turn loose." Then a woman knelt beside him and said, "You know, my friend, on the day I was converted, the very light of God hit me right in the face and knocked me down." Later the man explained, "During that time I was so busy and preoccupied, trying somehow to turn loose and at the same time hold on while looking around for the light of God to hit me in the face, that what I felt mostly was that I was confused."

Second, pluralism is rampant in our society. A century ago the United States was considered a "Christian nation." Because of the wholesale influx of non-Christian immigrants in the twentieth century, America is no longer considered by many as a totally Christian nation. Today it is reported that there are more Moslems in America than Methodists, more Buddhists than Episcopalians.

Pluralism holds that all religions are of equal value and are roads to God. Then the gospel is only relatively true. Other world religions are held to be different interpretations of the same God. Christians are not to evangelize or missionize but rather to be tolerant and understanding of other religions. In 1990 even the World Council of Churches declared that Christianity is not the one and only religion; the churches "need to move beyond a theology which confines salvation to the explicit personal commitment to Christ."

Today traditional Christians give one of three responses to pluralism:

(1) Exclusion. Non-Christian religions are invalid attempts to find God. Christ is the one and only way to salvation.

(2) Pluralism. All religions are valid and paths to God. Christianity is one among many ways to God. Though all religions are considered equal, Christianity is preferred.

(3) Inclusion. God is present and reveals himself in many ways, including the non-Christian religions. It does not really matter to what religion you hold.

Third, there is the menace of credulity. Many people are gullible and will believe anything and everything. One case of credulity deals with flying saucers. Roswell, New Mexico, in 1997 is observing the fiftieth anniversary of the alleged crash in 1947 of a flying saucer. The claim is that aliens from other planets visited the earth and crashed near Roswell. Thirty-four percent of Americans believe this even though the U.S. military concluded that a heap of debris was not from a saucer but from a downed weather balloon. Another case deals with the late Elvis Presley. Though a physician pronounced him dead and did an autopsy on his body and his grave is at his mansion, Graceland, in Memphis, millions of Americans consider him alive, living either in Hawaii or Michigan. They gather by the thousands each year to celebrate his birthday. A third case involved a strange configuration on a business building in Clearwater, Florida. To some it looked like a figure of the Virgin Mary. Within a couple of months millions came to look. They brought flowers, money, and prayers. They believed it was the Virgin Mary. A year later, the figure is still on the windows but hardly a person is there to behold it.

What You Can Believe

Every person is a believer. It is part of the human psyche to believe, but believe what? Each person has several options to believe. A bumper sticker says, "Honk, if you believe anything." "If you believe" — everyone is a believer. We only have to choose a belief.

Believe Nothing

A father described his teenage daughter as one who believes nothing but indulges in everything. When we believe nothing, anything goes!

A U.S. Navy radio man was convicted of selling government secrets to the Russians for $325,000. In sentencing him the judge remarked, "He betrayed his country for money because he believes in nothing."

Believing in nothing is known as nihilism. It is akin to atheism, except that an atheist believes that God does not exist. If one believes in nothing, the consequences are horrible. There are no guidelines or limits for behavior. With nothing to believe in, there is no security for the present and no hope for tomorrow. There is nothing to hold on to and no reason to live.

Believe Anything

A second opinion is to believe anything. One time an actress remarked that she believed in astrology. A friend was surprised. "I didn't know you believed in astrology." "Oh, yes, I believe in everything a little bit."

A couple visited a church of a different denomination. After the service they met one of the leaders of the church. They asked, "How does your church differ in doctrine?" He replied, "That's what is good about our church. You can believe anything you want."

Does it matter to parents to which church they send their children? One mother said that it did not make any difference to her whether her children became Buddhist so long as they believed in something and behaved morally.

One fallacy in the position to believe anything is the claim that it doesn't matter what you believe so long as you are sincere. Do we need to be reminded that Hitler was totally sincere when he fostered the Holocaust?

Another fallacy in this position is to hold to the view that it is not what you believe but what you do that counts. It is deeds, not creeds, that count, some say. Alex McCowen gives a one-man performance of the Gospel of Mark which he performs from memory without missing a word. One time he was asked why he was not a Christian. He explained, "It is what you do rather than what you believe."

Believe The Wrong Thing

Believing the wrong thing is known as heresy — falsehood, untruth, lies. Heresy has always plagued the upholders and proclaimers of truth. Jesus had the problem. He warned his disciples, "Beware of false prophets" (Matthew 7:15). Saint Paul fought against the Judaizers of his day. In Galatians he defended the gospel from them and uttered a curse against them: "But even if we or an angel from heaven should proclaim to you a gospel contrary to what we proclaimed to you, let that one be accursed!" (Galatians 1:8).

Throughout church history heretics had to be fought. Athanasius confronted Arius on the Trinity truth. Augustine fought Pelagius on the salvation issue. In the Middle Ages the Roman Church considered Protestants to be heretics and on Saint Bartholomew's Day she massacred 70,000 French Protestants. And don't forget that Martin Luther was excommunicated as a heretic!

Today the true Christian faith is threatened by heresies, cults, and sects that are built upon false teachings. A recent heresy is the New Age, which teaches anti-Christian doctrines such as reincarnation and pantheism. *Christianity Today* summed it up: "The New Age offers a Christ without a cross or physical resurrection, preaching a gospel without repentance or forgiveness, before an audience of potential equals without sin or shame who are in no peril of perdition." (April 29, 1991, p. 23)

The Church of Scientology is another heresy of our time. It was started by L. Ron Hubbard, a science fiction writer. *Time* magazine called it a "cult of greed." It is a secular program of mind manipulation, but it masquerades as a church.

The Goddess Sophia is a heresy of recent years dealing with feminist spirituality. She is considered the co-creator with God of the universe, a heavenly queen, and lover of God in a physical way. As a goddess she is worshiped and served by her believers.

Believe The Right Thing

How can we know what is the right thing to believe? Where do we get the truth to believe? Shall we go to church members for the answer? A true-false test was given to 4,371 church members regarding their beliefs. The results:

The Statement	Percentage True
(1) All people are sinners.	57
(2) Jesus is the Son of God	42
(3) Of many religions most lead to God.	42
(4) At birth a child is sinful.	63
(5) The gospel is God's rules for right living.	41
(6) We are saved by good works or intentions.	70

If you will look at the percentage, you will see that they are practically 50-50. Accordingly you should not get a unanimous answer from the average church membership. Where then shall we go for the truth?

Protestants hold that the sole source of truth for faith and life is the Bible. John Wesley stated it expertly: "We believe the written

Word of God to be the only and sufficient rule of both faith and practice." Why? Because the Bible is the recorded account of God's revelation completed in Jesus Christ, the Word Incarnate.

But the Bible can be a problem. It is a library of 66 books. It can be a confusing book with genealogies, liturgical directives, dietary laws, all of which are irrelevant to our age. The Bible is a book of progressive revelation with low and high points, and Christians do not accept the low points because they are superseded by the teachings of Jesus. What then in the Bible can we believe?

We turn to the church for help. The church's treasure is the Word of God, and she is the custodian of this treasure of truth which we can believe. In a marvelous and miraculous fashion the church has summarized and distilled the truth of the Bible in the creeds. To realize just what this means, suppose you were asked to reduce 1,151 pages of the Bible to 109 words without omitting one important truth. Could you do it?

It was done for us by the church in the Apostles' Creed. In a sermon of 1535 Martin Luther said, "This confession of faith [the Apostles' Creed] we did not make or invent, neither did the fathers of the church before us. But as the bee gathers honey from many a beautiful and delectable flower, so this creed has been collected in commendable brevity from the books of the beloved prophets and apostles, that is, from the entire Holy Scriptures."

Therefore, the right thing to believe is the truth of the Bible interpreted by Christ and summarized in the Apostles' Creed. The right thing to believe is whatever harmonizes with this creed.

Choose Your Belief

What do you believe? Are your beliefs in conformity with scriptural teachings? The best way to find out is by obeying Saint Paul's admonition: "Examine yourselves to see whether you are holding to your faith. Test yourselves" (2 Corinthians 13:5). Take the following test to learn what you are now believing. At the close of the series, take the test again and determine whether your answers were correct. In some cases you will need to check the *best* answer.

A creed is —
1. ___ a way of life.
2. _✓_ a statement of faith.
3. ___ a means of getting right with God.

The creeds were written by —
1. ___ Saint Paul.
2. ___ Jesus.
3. ___ the Church.
4. _✓_ unknown authors.

The Trinity means —
1. ___ we have three gods.
2. ___ God is divided into three persons.
3. ___ God is one with Jesus and the Holy Spirit as subordinates.
4. _✓_ God is one but manifests himself in three persons.

"I believe in God" means —
1. ___ I am an agnostic.
2. ___ I am a polytheist.
3. ___ I am an atheist.
4. _✓_ I am a monotheist.

God the Father implies —
1. ___ God is a male.
2. ___ God is a person.
3. _✓_ God is a personality.
4. _C_ God is a principle.

When God created the universe —
1. ___ He gave humanity permission to exploit it.
2. ___ He withdrew and let the world run itself.
3. _✓_ He made provision for our physical needs.

Jesus is —
1. _✓_ the Son of God.
2. ___ higher than the angels but lower than God.
3. ___ a man with a sense of God's presence.
4. ___ the same as God.

The Incarnation means —
1. ___ Jesus is totally human.
2. ___ Jesus is wholly God.
3. _✓_ Jesus is both God and man.
4. ___ Jesus is only a prophet of God.

Because Jesus died on the cross —
1. _✓_ we have access to God through forgiveness.
2. ___ we have an example on the cross.
3. ___ we can blame the Jews.
4. ___ we are free to live as we please.

It is correct to refer to the Holy Spirit as —
1. _✓_ it.
2. ___ he.
3. ___ she.

The Holy Spirit is God —
1. _3_ in the world.
2. _2_ in Christian believers.
3. ___ in all people.

The Holy Spirit comes to those who —
1. _✓_ receive the Word of God.
2. ___ live a good life.
3. ___ pay the tithe.
4. ___ attend worship services.

Christianity and other religions:
1. ___ most religions lead to God.
2. _✓_ all people, regardless of religion, are God's children.
3. ___ it is necessary to be a Christian to be saved.

The nature of humanity:
1. _✓_ at birth a child is sinful.
2. ___ regardless of religion, a person is of inherent worth.
3. ___ at baptism parents only dedicate a child to God.

The Gospel:
1. _✓_ God's rules for right living.
2. ___ with God's help, one can get right with God.
3. _3_ Christ died for our sins.

Chapter 2

The Faith Of The Creeds

What a Christian believes is expressed in the creeds. What is a creed? The word is a Latin word which is the first word of the Creed: *Credo,* meaning "I believe." A creed then is a statement of one's belief. It is a summary of beliefs based on the life and teachings of the historical Jesus. Christianity is not a religion about Jesus, but is based on the religion of the historical Jesus, upon the facts of his life. Christianity is not a philosophy of ideas so that it could exist even if there were no real Jesus. In the creeds Christian faith comes to an understanding. They explain the significance of the gospel.

The truth of the creeds is what the church teaches, preaches, and practices. The church as the body of Christ was led by the Spirit to express the true faith in the creeds. The church wrote the creeds, believes in the creeds, lives by the creeds, and confesses the creeds in worship every Sunday. Sunday after Sunday millions upon millions of Christians use the creeds, Apostles' or Nicene, to witness to their faith before God and the world. The creeds are not the work of any one particular church but the entire, universal church, including Roman Catholic, Protestant, and Orthodox churches. Through these creeds Christians are one in the faith.

The Creeds
Ecumenical Creeds

The ecumenical creeds are accepted by all churches (Roman Catholic, Eastern Orthodox, and Protestant) except a minority of Protestant churches such as Baptist and Quaker. What are these creeds?

1. Apostles' (c. 100 A.D.)

The Apostles' Creed is the oldest and shortest creed with only 109 words in the traditional version. Only the New Testament creed, "Jesus is Lord," is older. It is also the most often used — practically every Sunday, except for festivals and seasons when the Nicene Creed is confessed. Undoubtedly, it is the most universal statement of the Christian faith.

By 100 A.D. the Apostles' Creed became the basic statement of faith for the church. In the first century, it was the rule of faith for baptismal candidates. In 390 it became known as the Apostles' Creed, even though it was not written by the apostles but contained the beliefs of the apostles. An ancient legend has it that after Pentecost the apostles agreed on a summary of what they were going to preach. The summary was the Apostles' Creed. Yet, the creed did not reach its final form until the sixth or seventh century. Martin Luther held this creed in such high regard that he used it in his *Small Catechism* to teach families what a Christian believes. To this day the *Small Catechism* is used as the basis for youth and adult preparation for church membership in Lutheran churches.

2. Nicene (325-381 A.D.)

The Nicene Creed provides a fuller explanation of the Christian faith. It is called Nicene because a general council of the church, similar to Vatican II held in the 1960s, met in the city of Nicaea in Asia Minor. The Council was called to deal with the heresy of Arianism, which was a denial of the Trinity. The Nicene Creed goes into more detail than the Apostles' Creed on the Trinity and the person of Jesus.

A final version of the creed was formulated by another Council which met in Constantinople in 381 A.D. The creed is and has been from the start a topic of contention. In 598 a provincial church council meeting in Toledo, Spain, added the "filioque clause" which says that the Holy Spirit proceeded from the Father "and the Son." This added clause was accepted by the Western but not the Eastern church. It became one of the causes of the schism between East and West in 1064 A.D. Today the clause is still proving to be a stumbling block to closer relations with the Eastern Orthodox church. The Nicene Creed is familiar to most churchgoers in liturgical churches, because it is used in the worship service on festivals and certain seasons such as Advent, Christmas, Lent, and Easter.

3. Athanasian (428 A.D.)

This ecumenical creed is probably unknown to most Christians because it is seldom, if ever, used in worship services. It is probably not used because of its length. The Nicene Creed has eighteen printed lines, whereas the Athanasian has 69. It is difficult for congregations to use because of the creed's intricate and complex terms.

Though the creed carries the name of Athanasius, he did not write it. It was the product of the church of his time. The creed was named after him to honor him for his brave and forceful defense of the Trinity. Athanasius (289-373) was a bishop in Alexandria, Egypt.

The creed deals primarily with the Trinity and Jesus as the Son of God. At this time, the heresy of Arius was prominent. He taught that Jesus was not fully human or divine and that the Holy Spirit was not God but only a divine influence. The Athanasian Creed denounced these false teachings and upheld the doctrine of the Trinity. Luther's high regard for this creed was expressed: "I doubt, since the days of the Apostles, anything more important and more glorious has ever been written in the church of the New Testament."

Denominational Creeds

The ecumenical creeds state the general basic beliefs of the Church. How does one understand and interpret these broad truths? Most churches or denominations have felt the need for preparing their own creeds according to their understanding of the scriptures.

Moreover, the ecumenical creeds do not deal with many lesser important teachings. What is the Christian teaching about the nature of humanity, the gospel ministry, the Atonement, or the Second Coming? How is a person born again? What is the meaning of justification by grace through faith? How are we to understand the sacraments?

Churches which have prepared their own creeds do not do so in opposition to the ecumenical creeds, but as supplements to them.

These churches are known as confessional churches because they hold to their confessions or creeds. By their creeds they are confessing the gospel as they understand it. Among the denominational creeds are —

The Augsburg Confession — Lutheran, 1530
The Thirty-nine Articles — Episcopal, 1563
The Heidelberg Catechism — Reformed, 1563
The Westminster Confession — Presbyterian, 1647
The Twenty-five Articles of Religion — Methodist, eighteenth century.

Individual Creed

The ecumenical and denominational creeds do not take the place of the individual's confession of faith. Each Christian needs a personal creed which harmonizes with the ecumenical and denominational creeds. The creed serves as an expression of one's faith. One has an experience with Christ and then tries to explain what happened. A creed does not save a person. One is already saved by grace through faith in Christ. The creeds are not like cookie cutters that stamp out little Christians all of one mold. One does not become a Christian by merely giving intellectual assent to a creed. Each person should be able to write a statement of belief. This becomes one's creed. Can you sit down and write your personal creed in no more than 109 words like that of the traditional Apostles' Creed?

A Threefold Purpose

Why bother with creeds? Why not let each Christian decide what to believe? The creeds are of great value to each Christian for they fulfill a threefold purpose.

Definition

One purpose of the creeds is to define the Christian faith. What does a Christian believe or what should a Christian believe to be called a Christian? Are the personal beliefs in harmony with the scriptures and the church's teachings? Can a Christian believe in reincarnation? In pantheism? In astrology?

A group of college students of various denominations had a long discussion about what they believed. When it was over, a coed came to the chaplain with a protest. She complained, "The Roman Catholic knew what she believed. The Jew knew where he stood. The Jehovah's Witness was positive about her beliefs. As a Methodist, I am embarrassed because I did not know what I believe. Why didn't I know?"

One woman was seeking truth. She had some questions she wanted answered. Eventually she ended up with the Jehovah's Witnesses. Why end there? She explained, "I tried seven different churches and none of them could answer my questions. When I met with the Witnesses, they could give me an answer."

Here is where the creeds can help us. As long as the creeds are known and understood, no Christian should ever be unable to tell or explain what a Christian believes. Holding to the creeds, a Christian can say, "This is what I believe and I know it is the truth because it comes from the Bible."

Defense

The creeds were prepared to defend the Christian faith against the heresies prevailing at the time: Gnosticism, Arianism, and the Judaizers. Throughout the centuries heresies have plagued the church. They are as prevalent today as they were in the first century. The creeds counteract the false teaching and declare the biblical truth. The creeds are our sure defense.

Suppose you see a white Volkswagon parked on a city street. On its side is painted, "Reverend Sun Myung Moon is the living Christ." How would you defend the truth that Christ alone is the Messiah?

A fellow worker refuses to work on Saturdays, because he claims that the true sabbath is Saturday and not Sunday. He claims that working on Saturday breaks the commandment and is therefore a sin. How would you defend Sunday as the sabbath?

Since baptism is considered necessary for salvation, two young men, who come to your home uninvited, claim that if your ancestors were not baptized and therefore not saved, you could be baptized for them. Then at once they would enter the presence of God for eternity. What would be your defense that baptism is only for the living?

An independent preacher comes to town, puts up a revival tent, and preaches: There is no such thing as hell. The soul is not immortal. When a Christian dies, he/she does not go directly to heaven. No one is born in sin. How would the creed respond to these teachings?

In each case, the defense you give is the creed. The teachings of the sects and cults are counterfeit. How can you tell the difference between the genuine and the counterfeit teachings? The American Banking Association trains bank tellers how to detect counterfeit bills. Strangely, no one studies counterfeit money nor handles it. The tellers do not listen to lectures denouncing counterfeiters. Rather, they handle real money hour after hour, day after day, until they become so familiar with genuine bills that, when a counterfeit comes, they can detect the difference. It is the same with our use of the creed. When we become familiar with the creed and use it regularly, we will be able to detect heresy and reject it for the truth of the creed.

Declaration

A third purpose of the creeds is declaration. Before ascending to heaven, Jesus urged his disciples to be his witnesses in the world. We are to let the world know the truth about God, life, and salvation. If we are to tell the world about the truth of God, what shall we say and how shall we say it?

The creeds enable us to fulfill Jesus' command to tell the world the truth. We use the creeds for a personal and corporate witnessing before God and the world. For this reason many churches use the creed in worship services. After hearing the Word of God read and preached, the congregation responds by confessing the faith in the creeds and as they just heard in the Bible readings. Saying the creed is a positive, fearless declaration of our Christian faith. Many church members do not understand this use of the creed in worship. Many say the creed softly with bowed head and folded hands as though the creed were a prayer. Indeed, it does end with "Amen" just as a prayer does, but in this case the "Amen" is an expression of affirmation as though to say, "This is most certainly true." Saying the creed in worship is much like saying the pledge of allegiance to the flag. As loyal Americans, we put our hands on our hearts, look at the flag, and proudly and loudly say, "I pledge allegiance ..." So it should be when we confess our faith in saying the creed: stand at attention, look at the cross, and with conviction say, "I believe ..." When the devil and the ungodly world hear Christians with one voice confessing the truth of the creed, they tremble!

In the old days, a conservative college required students to attend chapel each day. The same order of service was used daily. For the sake of variety, they decided to change the order by omitting the Apostles' Creed on Tuesdays and Thursdays. One student in the habit of saying the creed began on Tuesday to say, "I believe in God ..." A fellow student poked him in the ribs and whispered, "Not on Tuesdays and Thursdays." For true Christians the creed is for every day. Luther taught that a Christian should confess the Apostles' Creed eight times a day.

The Faith Of The Creeds

Your Own Creed

You have learned about various creeds: ecumenical, denominational, and personal. Now is the time for you to write your own creed: What do you believe about the Christian faith?

Can you limit your creed to 109 words as does the Apostles' Creed?

When you finish writing your creed, check to see if you covered every chief doctrine.

Personal Creeds In The New Testament

Review the following personal creeds:

Matthew 16:16 — The most famous of all confessions of faith.

Mark 9:24 — Can one believe and not believe at the same time?

John 4:29 — The confession of a pagan woman.

John 9:35-38 — The belief of a healed blind youth.

John 11:25-27 — What was Martha's belief?

Your Own Defense

How would you defend the Christian faith when confronted with the claim that the Rev. Moon is the Messiah; that the Sabbath falls on Saturday; that the living can be baptized for the dead; that an Evangelist preaches there is no hell? Present your defense to the class.

Chapter 3

The Holy Trinity

Christians of all denominations love to sing Reginald Heber's "Holy, holy, holy, Lord God Almighty ... God in three persons, blessed Trinity." All may like to sing it, but how many understand what they are singing about — the blessed Trinity? We need to understand it because it is the central doctrine of the Christian faith, for all Christian teachings find their center in the Trinity. This one unique doctrine identifies Christianity from all other religions. Jews and Moslems see the Trinity as a blasphemous insult to the one God beside whom there can be no other. Today's feminists protest against the Trinity and call for its rejection because, they claim, it perpetuates the symbolic domination of males as the true image of God as Father, Son, and Holy Spirit.

The content of the ecumenical creeds is built on the structure of the Trinity. The Trinity is simply stated: God is one but he manifests himself in three persons: Father, Son, and Holy Spirit. You will notice that in the Apostles' and Nicene Creeds a paragraph is given to each person. This is in accord with English grammar. A sentence contains a complete thought. A group of sentences makes a paragraph dealing with one subject. Change the subject and you are to begin a new paragraph. The first paragraph of the creeds concerns God the Father, even though in the Apostles' Creed the paragraph consists of only one sentence. The second paragraph deals with God the Son and the third with the Holy Spirit. These paragraphs of the creed are known as "articles."

Is the Trinity a biblical or church teaching? New Testament scholars assure us that the New Testament contains no doctrine of the Trinity. Although one cannot find a specific text on the Trinity, there are many references in the Bible to the Trinity. For instance, at Jesus' baptism there were the Father's voice, the Son's presence, and the Spirit's descent in the form of a dove (Matthew 3:13-

17). Paul uses the Trinity in the form of a benediction: "The grace of the Lord Jesus Christ and the love of God and the fellowship of the Holy Spirit be with you all" (2 Corinthians 13:14).

Understanding The Trinity

To understand the creeds we need to understand the Trinity because the structure of the creeds is the Trinity.

The most serious heresy of the fourth century was Arianism. For a half century the church was split over the controversy of the Trinity. Arius was a priest in Alexandria, Egypt. He quarrelled with his bishop's sermon on the divinity of Christ. The controversy spread to such an extent that Emperor Constantine called a Council to meet in Nicaea in 325. It was attended by 318 bishops from all sections of the church.

The Arians held to the view that God was one God who was unknowable, inconceivable, unreachable, and unchangeable. This transcendent God could not have taken human form in Jesus. Thus, Christ was a subordinate, created creature who stood between the world and an unknowable God. Therefore, Jesus was not God, nor was he the Spirit. If Jesus were only a creature of God and not God, he could not reveal God nor redeem the world. Then the worship of Jesus as a creature would be idolatry.

Athanasius, a bishop for 47 years in Alexandria, defended the concept of God as Trinity and is largely responsible for the defeat of Arius' views. A Council of 150 Eastern bishops condemned Arianism at Constantinople in 381. Since this was a Council of the East only, the entire church met in 451 at Chalcedon to confirm the Nicene Creed, which defeated the theology of Arius and defended the Trinitarian view. Thus, the Nicene Creed finally became the official creed for the whole church by passing through Nicaea, Constantinople, and Chalcedon.

The crux of the controversy centered on the question of whether Jesus was truly God or only a creature of God as held by Arius. It came down to a single Greek word, *homoousias* or *homoiousias*. *Homoousias* meant Jesus was of the same substance as God or oneness with God. *Homoiousias* meant Jesus was *like* or similar to God, that Jesus was divine but not deity.

The problem of the Trinity is how God can be one and yet be manifested in three persons as Father, Son, and Spirit. This is also a problem for non-Christian religions. A Protestant seminary class was taken to a synagogue to observe a Friday evening service. A lay member of the synagogue welcomed the group saying, "In welcoming you to our synagogue, I want to call your attention to some of the differences between us Jews and you Christians. The most basic is that while you believe in three Gods, we believe in one."

Apparently the Jewish layman did not understand that Christians also believe in one God. Saint Paul wrote to the Corinthian church: "There is no God but one. Yet for us there is one God, the Father, from whom are all things and for whom we exist" (1 Corinthians 8:4, 6). This one God manifests himself in three persons. We need to understand that "person" does not mean an independent person, for this would make three Gods. "Person" is used as in the characters of a drama, *dramatis personae*. The "person" is a character who plays a role. In Greek ancient drama one actor/actress could play several characters by putting on different masks. Some years ago Planters Peanuts had an advertising gimmick. A man was dressed as a peanut from head to hips, wore glasses and a high top hat, and walked with a cane back and forth in front of the store. Suppose that the next day he wore a pecan mask and the next day he wore a walnut. In each case it was the same man but as three different persons. As Christians, then, we do not have three Gods but one God who expresses himself in three persons. There is but one substance, and that substance is God as Father, Son, and Holy Spirit. Each person is a real personality without saying that each person is only an expression of one person. To say this is to fall into the error of Modalism. Each person of the Trinity is God, but each person has his own individuality without becoming separate entities. Also, each person has his own work: Father — creation; Son — redemption; Holy Spirit — sanctification.

How can an average person understand the Trinity? How can there be three in one? You say that God is one and at the same time you say that each person of the Trinity is God. Does that not make three Gods? We must admit that it is a paradox and seemingly a contradiction that goes against all logic. The story is told of a man who had a heart attack in a store while he was shopping. Thinking that the man was dying, the store manager called a priest to administer last rites. Cardinal Cushing at the time was the priest. He knelt down beside the fallen man and asked, "Do you believe in God the Father, God the Son, and God the Holy Spirit?" The man roused a little, opened one eye, looked at all standing around, and said, "Here I am dying and the guy is asking me riddles." Ultimately the Trinity is a mystery, a riddle. No one has ever been able to explain it adequately. But this should not bother us, for there are many things in life we cannot understand, yet we live with them and by them. You probably have a microwave oven. Do you understand how it can heat food red-hot and yet the oven stays cool? You are probably reading this book with the aid of an electric light, but can you explain what electricity is? We may not be able to understand or explain the Trinity, but we do know God loves us, cares for us, and saves us when we repent and believe in Christ as Savior.

Aids To Understanding

Various analogies have been used to help us understand the Trinity, but not one is adequate. According to legend, Saint Patrick went to Ireland and preached to the king. A snag occurred when the king could not understand the Trinity. Patrick tried various explanations, but the king was not persuaded to accept the Trinity. In desperation Patrick plucked a shamrock and asked, "How many plants do I have here?" The king answered, "One." "Yes," continued Patrick , "but it has three leaves — Father, Son, and Holy Spirit." This convinced the king. Shortly thereafter he was baptized.

Personal relationships can also be an analogy. A person can be one person but at the same time three different persons in a relationship. For instance, a man can be a son, a husband, and a father. He is the same person, but not the same person to each of the three. So God is one but in three persons.

Science is sometimes used to explain the Trinity. Water is the substance, but it can be expressed as liquid, as a solid (ice), or a vapor (steam). The substance is the same. As liquid, solid, or vapor it is still water. God is the basic substance, water, but he comes to the world as Father, Son, and Spirit.

Though we use various analogies to explain the Trinity, not one of them is a perfect illustration or explanation. We must be content to let the Trinity be a mystery and accept it by faith as a central biblical teaching. Now we see the Trinity through a glass darkly but in heaven it will become clear to us.

The Shield Of The Trinity

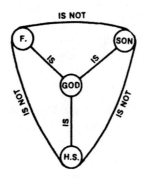

The mystery and the meaning of the Trinity are shown in the ancient shield of the Trinity. What does this symbol say about the Trinity? Let us begin with the center of the figure — "God." Who or what is God? God is in the center of our lives as reality, essence, life, being, the *summum bonum*, our ultimate concern. God is because he IS. When Moses asked God to explain who he was, God simply answered, "I am who I am" (Exodus 3:14). To say anything more about God is to limit him. Anything additional you might say about God is only an attribute. If you say, "God is love," you are correct, but God is also truth and justice. It is like looking at the sun and the rays of the sun. The sun is the essence of God and the attributes are the rays of the sun. To understand God fully, we would have to know the infinite attributes and qualities of God. Since this is impossible, we can say God is Being, Reality, Life, Essence, Spirit.

Practical Implications

This basic understanding of God has practical implications for us today. First, God is above and beyond all we can say or think. No one can put God in a corner or in a box and claim to know all there is to know about him. Paul wrote, "O the depth of the riches and wisdom and knowledge of God! How unsearchable are his judgments and how inscrutable his ways!" (Romans 11:33). To try to see or touch God means death, for he is infinite, incomprehensible, and unapproachable. When God came to Mount Sinai, the people were warned not to touch the mountain lest they die (Exodus 19:10-12). When David was bringing the ark of the covenant to Jerusalem, Uzzah was smitten with death for touching the ark, for it was the symbol of God's presence. When a son of Karl Barth, considered the greatest theologian of the twentieth century, was asked to address a convention, he saw above the speaker's stand a banner saying, "God is other people." When it was time for his address, he went to the sign and put a comma after "other" so that it read, "God is other, people." That was his message and he sat down without saying another word. God is the totally other. When we confront God in all of his glory, majesty, truth, and power, we respond with adoration, awe, and reverence.

Again, this understanding of God should solve the problem heard in the Feminist movement of our day. Nonsexist language is a concern of many. The avant-garde leaders insist upon calling God "mother" and refer to him as "she" or "parent." Since God is Spirit, he cannot be a "he," "she," or "it." God is not a sexual being, neither male nor female. Why then did Jesus teach us to call God "father"? It is not because God is masculine, but he performs a masculine role in terms of creation, protection, preservation, and providence. The feminine factor of the Christian faith is the church. She is our mother. John Calvin once said, "If you do not have the church as your mother, you cannot have God as your father." Believers in Christ are the children of the bridegroom, Jesus, and his bride, the church. In Christian symbolism, the symbol of the church is a she, and the ship is always referred to as a "she."

Take another look at the shield of the Trinity. It tells us who God is: he is God the Father; he is God the Son; he is God the

38

Spirit. Each one is God. But the shield gets us in trouble when we see that the Father is not the Son; the Son is not the Spirit; the Spirit is not the Father. If each were the other, there would not be three separate persons. Each person of the Trinity has his own personality and work. While we have three persons, we have but one God. "Hear, O Israel: The Lord our God is one Lord" (Deuteronomy 6:4). As we have seen, this constitutes the mystery of the Holy Trinity.

Characteristics Of The Trinity

Co-eternal

The three persons of the Trinity are co-eternal. This means that each person is eternal. There never was nor will there ever be a time when the persons of the Trinity did not exist. God the Father is by nature eternal, from everlasting to everlasting. "In the beginning God...." In the beginning of the universe God created the heavens and the earth, but it does not mean the beginning of God.

Then God the Son, Jesus, was supposed to have come into existence when he was born in 4 B.C. This overlooks the pre-existence of Jesus. The Bible speaks of Jesus as the Alpha and Omega, the beginning and end (Revelation 1:8). The author of Hebrews says, "Jesus Christ is the same yesterday, today, and forever" (Hebrews 13:8). In John's Gospel, Jesus, the Word of God, was in the beginning and the world was made through him.

Some may think that the Holy Spirit came into existence at Pentecost, 30 A.D. Contrary to this view, the Spirit is God and God is eternal. The Bible tells us that the Spirit of God created the universe (Genesis 1:2). The Spirit existed before Jesus, for he spoke through the prophets, caused the virgin birth, and descended on Jesus. On Pentecost the Spirit came to the disciples to guide them into truth and to empower them to witness to Christ.

Co-equal

A second characteristic of the Trinity is that the three persons are co-equal. This truth needs to be known, for the common opinion puts God as top priority, the greatest of the three persons. Jesus supposedly is subordinate because he was limited by his humanity.

The Spirit is supposed to be less than Christ because he comes partially into a believer's heart. In contrast, the Bible teaches us that Jesus is no less than the Father, and the Spirit has the same power as the Father. Each person of the Trinity is equal in authority, power, and grace.

Wrong view:

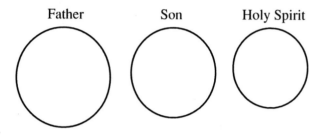

Correct view:

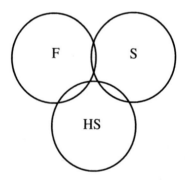

Co-operative

The persons of the Trinity are cooperative. They are not in competition with each other. When we call upon the Father, at the same time we get the help of the Son and the Spirit. Each person is able to help us. Each one loves us and cares for us. All three work together for our salvation by doing the work of creation, redemption, and sanctification.

An Overview Of The Trinity

Before we make a detailed study of the Apostles' Creed, an overview may help us to get a perspective.

Article	Person	Nature of Person	Area Of Person	Work Of Person	Symbol
I	Father	Transcendence (God beyond us)	Universe	Creation (What God did)	Hand
II	Son	Incarnation (God with us)	Jesus	Redemption (What God did *for* us)	Lamb
III	Spirit	Immanence (God in us)	Believer	Sanctification (What God does *in* us)	Dove

Notes:

1. The three articles with the three persons are in three paragraphs, one for each person.

2. Nature of the person: Transcendence belongs to the Father, for he is invisible, incomprehensible, unknowable. He is the totally other. Incarnation deals with Jesus, the Word made flesh. God the Son became a human as Jesus of Nazareth. Immanence deals with the Holy Spirit, who as the third person of the Trinity dwells in the heart and mind of a believer. He is a personal God who lives in a believer.

3. Area of the person: The Father is universal as the Creator. He is greater than his creation. He is everywhere. The Son is located in Jesus of Nazareth. Jesus said, "The Father and I are one." The Spirit abides in the believer who receives the Spirit when he is born again.

4. Work of the person: God the Father's work is the creation of the universe. This is our Father's world. He sustains and preserves it. This is what God did. The Work of the Son is redemption wrought for us on the cross. This is what God did for us. Sanctification is the work of the Spirit. He makes us Christians by calling us to believe. By grace we are the children of God by justification. Now the Spirit makes us what we are.

5. Symbol: The traditional symbol for the Father is a hand of God pointing from the heavens to earth — the creative touch of life. The Lamb refers to Jesus as the sacrificial Lamb whose blood was shed for the sins of the world. John the Baptist said about Jesus, "Behold the lamb of God who takes away the sin of the world." When Jesus was baptized, the Spirit came upon him like a dove. Since then the dove has symbolized the Holy Spirit coming to us.

The Church's Use Of The Trinity

Most churches make much of the Trinity. At least once every Sunday the Trinity is mentioned or used in various ways. There are hymns on the Trinity. When the offering is received, some churches sing the Doxology:

> Praise God from whom all blessings flow,
> Praise him, all creatures here below,
> Praise him above, ye heavenly hosts,
> Praise Father, Son, and Holy Ghost.

When a Psalm is used in worship, the congregation usually sings the Gloria Patri: "Gloria be to the Father and to the Son and to the Holy Ghost. As it was in the beginning, is now, and ever shall be. World without end. Amen." The Gloria is used to give a Christian interpretation of a Hebrew poem. The worship service usually begins with an invocation such as "In the Name of the Father and of the Son and of the Holy Spirit." The triune God is called to be present with his people and indicates that this assembly is a religious service. The worship service may end with the Trinity spoken in the benediction, such as the Aaronic Benediction with its three parts:

> The Lord bless you and keep you.
> The Lord make his face shine upon you and be gracious unto you.
> The Lord look upon you with favor and give you peace.

The Trinity is used in the Sacrament of Baptism. Jesus directed that we should baptize "in the name of the Father and of the Son and of the Holy Spirit." To be baptized in only one or two names of God would be improper. In recent times three students at Liberty University in Lynchburg, Virginia, were expelled because they were spreading the belief that converts should be baptized only in the name of Jesus and not in the name of Father, Son, and Holy Ghost.

In prayer we use the Trinity. We direct our prayer to the Father through the Son by the power of the Spirit. To get to the Father we must go through Jesus, for Jesus said, "No man comes to the Father but by me" (John 14:6). The Spirit gives us power to pray, teaches us to pray, and prays for us. Paul wrote, "We do not know how to pray as we ought, but the Spirit himself intercedes for us with sighs too deep for words" (Romans 8:26).

The Trinity appears in the church year. It is observed the Sunday after Pentecost Sunday. Before Vatican II, Trinity was a season lasting for almost a half year. Now the season is called Pentecost.

Symbols Of The Trinity

Symbols of the Trinity can be found in many churches, especially older church buildings. Some churches carry the name of Trinity, such as "Trinity Lutheran Church." Trinity symbols can be found in stained-glass windows, on paraments, and on chancel furnishings. Some of the common symbols of the Trinity:

Equilateral triangle:

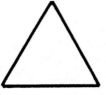

Triangle with a circle to represent the eternal Trinity:

43

Three interlocking circles:

The trefoil:

The fleur-de-lis with its three parts:

Three connecting fishes in a circle:

The Holy Trinity

The Trinity

1. Why is the first paragraph of the Apostles' Creed only a sentence? Is this faulty grammar?

2. How can God be one and yet three persons, each claiming to be God? Is this a contradiction?

3. How do you define or describe the Trinity?

The Trinity In Analogies

Please fill in the blanks below:

1. Human relationships: One person can be a _____, _____, and _____, but yet be one and the same person.

2. Physical world: Water can be a _____, _____, and _____.

The Trinity In Worship

Please fill in the blanks below:

1. Invocation: "In the name of the _____, _____, and _____."

2. Gloria Patri: "Glory be to the _____, _____, and _____."

3. Doxology: "Praise _____, _____, and _____."

4. Baptism: "I baptize you in the name of the _____, _____, and _____."

5. Benediction: "The grace of our _____, the love of _____, and the communion of the _____ be with you all."

The Trinity Symbols

Go into your church and/or chapel and copy the symbols of the Trinity you find there. Bring your "art work" for display to the next session.

God The Father

The First Article Of The Apostles' Creed

Traditional Version
   "I believe in God the Father Almighty, maker of heaven and earth."

Ecumenical Version
   "I believe in God, the Father Almighty, creator of heaven and earth."

Chapter 4

I Believe

When Vince Lombardi came to take over as coach of the Green Bay Packers, he held his first meeting with the players. He opened the training session by saying, "We will begin with the fundamentals of football." Holding up a football, he continued, "Now this is what you call a football." One of the veteran players responded, "Coach, will you please run through that again? I didn't get it!"

In our study of the Apostles' Creed we will be dealing with the fundamentals of our Christian faith. The creed gives us the simple basics that every true Christian confesses as his/her personal faith. The Apostles' Creed is the ABC's of our Christian religion, the very minimum one needs to believe. Each of the 109 words of the creed is essential and packed with meaning. To get the full meaning and truth of the creed, we will look at almost every word in it.

A Personal Confession

The very first word of the creed is the first personal pronoun, "I." It is not "we," as though this were a corporate confession. Rather, it is an individual and personal confession usually given in a corporate experience of worship. Of course, one can use the creed for private devotions. And the first word of the creed is not "they." This creed does not refer to others of the past or of the future, but to each of us in the present. "I believe" is present tense — here and now.

When we say "I" believe, we are indicating what the nature of Christianity is. It is a personal relationship with the triune God, a relationship established by faith in Christ who makes us acceptable to God the Father. If Christianity is to be real, it is necessary for each person to enter this relationship. Christianity is not a liturgy, not a hierarchy of clergy, a physical church plant, nor a theology or an ethical code. These may be a part of the Christian religion, but they are secondary and nonessential. The heart of our faith is the relationship with Christ. This was demonstrated at Caesarea Philippi when Jesus asked his disciples what people were saying about his identity. But it was not what "they" say but "Who do *you* say that I am?" A Christian says with Peter, "You are the Christ" (Matthew 16:13-16).

In a sense then, it is not really the Apostles' Creed, but my very own creed — John's creed or Mary's creed. If our Christian religion is a personal relationship with God, the creed has to be my very own. No one can enter into this relationship but me. No one can take my place. There can be no surrogate nor substitute. No one can be a Christian by proxy. In *The Road Less Travelled* Scott Peck writes, "Our religion must be a wholly personal one, forged entirely through the fire of our questioning and doubting in the crucible of our own experience of reality."

There are some things that only you can do. No one can take a bath for you or take your medicine to get you well. No one can die for you. Martin Luther said, "Every Christian must do his own believing just as he must do his own dying." You cannot be absent when death comes, as Woody Allen said, "It's not that I am afraid to die. I just don't want to be there when it happens." Likewise, no one can do your loving or believing for you. In the parable of the five wise and five foolish maidens, the foolish ones allowed their lamps to go out. When the bridegroom came, the foolish ones rushed to the wise girls and begged them to give them some of their oil. The wise refused and told them to buy oil from the dealers (Matthew 25:1-13). This was not selfish or mean on the part of the wise women. It is a fact that we cannot borrow the oil of faith or use someone else's faith. Faith cannot be borrowed, purchased, stolen, or inherited. We will not get to heaven because our parents and/or grandparents were faithful Christians.

Christianity, therefore, is an individual affair. It is a private and personal relationship with God in Christ. Alfred N. Whitehead said, "Religion is what one does with one's solitariness." God calls us to be Christians not by groups or *en masse*, but one by one. He called one man, Abraham, to be the father of a nation; another man, Moses, to lead a people out of slavery; one woman, Mary, to be the mother of the Savior; and one rebel, Paul, to plant the church in the ancient world.

Basically, Christianity is not a corporate affair as religion was in the Old Testament. By being a citizen of Israel, a person automatically became one of God's chosen people. It was a covenant with the people as a nation. An individual shared in the covenant through circumcision. Later Jeremiah in the sixth century announced a new covenant, which would be made with each person by having the Law written on the heart of each person. That promise was fulfilled in Jesus' new covenant made with each believer. Jesus dealt primarily with individuals. To each he said, "Come, follow me." Indeed, the church is a corporate body of God's people. But the Body consists of individual members brought and kept together by the Holy Spirit.

Establishing A Relationship
Since the Christian religion is based on a relationship with God through faith in Jesus Christ, how and when is that relationship established? The relationship begins when a person is baptized regardless of the age of the person. Baptism is God's official and objective act of adopting us as his children. He accepts us for Jesus' sake. We are given the Holy Spirit and made members of his Kingdom. The requirements for entering this relationship are repentance and faith. The water of baptism acts like a seal of the covenant relationship. Luther said that when his faith faltered that he was God's child, and he crept on his hands and knees to the baptismal font, where God accepted him originally.

In the event a person was baptized as an infant, the time comes when the child is of mature reason and can answer for him/herself. The church calls it confirmation. The promises of baptism are confirmed. The youth repeats the promises made by the sponsors of infant baptism. For the first time the youth publicly declares faith in Christ and promises loyalty to Christ and his church.

How the relationship occurs is not the same in all cases. There is the immediate style of conversion. The person is usually an adult who has had an emotional experience with God or Jesus. Like Saint Paul on the way to Damascus, the experience was sudden: he fell e, he heard a voice, he saw a blinding light, he was nd. The experience turned him to Christ who called him rvant and apostle. There is a complete turnaround in life to Christ, from sin to holiness, from disobedience to service. Though not all Christians have had this experience, it is valid and authentic.

On the other hand, the relationship can be a gradual one of growth into the relationship over the years. In my own case, I did not have an emotional conversion, but a slow, gradual evolution into an ever closer relationship. For twelve days I was not a Christian. I was born on December 19 and baptized on the following January 1. But over the years the faith has matured and the relationship with Christ has grown closer. This method is also valid and an authentic experience of relationship.

It is one thing to establish a relationship with God but it is another to maintain and increase that relationship. This is done by daily prayer, daily Bible reading, faithfully receiving the Sacraments, and weekly worship. The relationship with God can also be strengthened by Christian fellowship and unselfishly giving service to both the church and the world.

Personal Benefits

When a person says in the creed, "I," there is a personal experience. It indicates that you came to know, love, and believe in Jesus as Lord and Savior. You accepted Christ, surrendered your life, and committed to serve him the rest of your life. After physicist Arthur Compton addressed an assembly of college students, a student addressed him, "How can you really prove to me what it is like to be a Christian?" Dr. Compton asked for an orange. As everyone watched, he peeled it and began to eat it. Then he asked the student, "Do you know what the orange tasted like?" The student replied, "Of course I don't. Only the person who ate it can tell that." "So it is with Christianity," Compton concluded. "You must taste it yourself."

Job was one who tasted his faith in God. After his argument with God, he said, "I had heard of thee by the hearing of the ear, but now my *eye* sees thee" (Job 42:5). When Thomas confronted the resurrected Christ, he exclaimed, "My Lord and my God" (John 20:28). When Luther was preparing his university Bible lecture in the Black Tower, he read, "The just shall live by faith." For him then the heavens opened and for the first time he understood the meaning of the gospel. He said that he felt like he was born anew.

When you say, "I" believe, you have an assurance, confidence, and conviction about your relationship with God. By virtue of your faith, you know you are God's child, that you are saved, and that you are bound for heaven. Because of this "I," Paul could say with certainty, "I know whom I have believed" (2 Timothy 1:12). Faith became personal for John Wesley, who, at a prayer meeting on Aldersgate Street, said, "I did know that Christ has taken away my sins, even mine, and has saved me from the law of sin and death."

This "I" of the creed confesses that you have committed your life to the triune God. As a result of your faith, your life is under new management. You gave your heart to Christ and only you can do that. John Calvin's crest consisted of a flaming heart in an outstretched hand with the words, "My heart I give Thee, Lord, eagerly and sincerely."

Only Believe

As though I were the only person in the world, I stand alone and say "I." I what? I think? I demand? I object? Before God, the church, and the world, a Christian says in the Apostles' Creed, "I believe." What do I believe? In whom do I believe?

Maybe I don't believe in anything or anyone. It is possible I can be so confused that I do not know what to believe. A student at Emory University told this story. When a student is a freshman, he/she is a Republican. By the time he/she is a sophomore, he/she is a Democrat. In the third year the student is a Marxist. But in the last year, he/she is nothing. By then the student is so confused by various professors and courses taken that he/she does not know what to believe.

A true Christian is one who says with Paul, "I know whom I have believed." What a Christian minimally believes is contained in the Apostles' Creed. A Christian is a believer. The church is a society of believers. In Hendersonville, North Carolina, there is a commercial building outside of which is this sign: "Faith Associates, Inc." This sign would be appropriate outside a church, because Christian people are faith associates.

Fundamental Faith

Faith for a Christian is absolutely essential and indispensable. Next to grace, it is the most important element in life. G. K. Chesterton once said it was more important for a landlady to know what a boarder believes than to know the amount of his weekly paycheck.

Without faith there can be no Christianity, no church, no salvation. Without faith God in Christ cannot help or save us. When Jesus came to Nazareth, his hometown, he could not help any of the people. In other places he could heal the sick, open the eyes of the blind, and cleanse lepers, but not in Nazareth. Why? Because they had no faith in him. Matthew reports, "He did not do many mighty works there because of their unbelief" (Matthew 13:58).

Our salvation depends on faith. When the Philippian jailer wanted to know what he must do to be saved, Paul told him, "Believe on the Lord Jesus and you will be saved" (Acts 16:31). This coincides with what Paul wrote to the Ephesians, "By grace you have been saved through faith" (Ephesians 2:8). It is not that faith saves us. Grace alone saves us as demonstrated on the cross. Faith simply accepts the gift of salvation. It is the hand that reaches out to take the gift to oneself.

Healing depends on faith. Without faith in Christ's power and willingness to heal, we cannot be healed physically or emotionally. A woman, suffering from a twelve-year hemorrhage, touched Jesus' garment and was healed. How did Jesus explain this miracle? He told her, "Your faith has made you well" (Matthew 9:22).

None of us has any idea what power is at our disposal if we have faith. The smallest amount of faith can do wonders. Hear Jesus' own words: "If you have faith as a grain of mustard seed, nothing will be impossible to you" (Matthew 17:20). Note the contrast: the minimum of faith has maximum power. Faith has greater power than a nuclear explosion, because faith is the power only for good.

Faith is the key that unlocks the power of God, and no one nor anything can equal the power of God.

Faith is indispensable not only for earthly but also for eternal life. At the death of Lazarus, Martha was comforted when Jesus said, "He who believes in me, though he die, yet shall he live" (John 11:25). To this day at the funeral of one who died believing in Christ, the mourners can truthfully say, "He is not dead but is alive in heaven."

Since faith is so indispensable for a Christian, it is absolutely essential to keep the faith. One may never fall from the grace of God but one can easily lose faith. If faith is lost; all is lost. The power is gone. Death reigns. We are lost in sin. In Revelation, the ascended Christ admonishes the church, "Be faithful unto death" (Revelation 2:10). The question for each of us is not whether we have faith, but will we have faith until death?

False Faces Of Faith

When I was a child, at Halloween we put on masks that we called "false faces." The mask of a gorilla or a devil was a false face because, happily, it was not our real face. Faith can also put on false faces. Not all faith is worthy to be held. In writing to Timothy, Paul speaks of people who have the form but not the power of religion. They have a "counterfeit faith" (2 Timothy 3:8). It is really then not a matter of having faith, but of having true faith. In order to determine whether our faith is genuine, we need to look at some of the false faces of faith.

One false face is blind faith. With a blind faith we close our eyes to reality. We refuse to use our minds. It is like a boy's definition of faith: "Faith is believing what you know ain't so." Or as a little lad said, "If my father says it is so, it's so, even if it ain't so." Gina Lollobrigida has a statue of Saint Christopher in her car and puts faith in him to protect her on the highways. Despite Pope Paul's official decree that the saint may never have existed, she insists, "I don't care. He saved my life when my car crashed last February."

Another false face of faith is demanding a sign that what you believe is real and true. We want confirmation of our faith. In Jesus' day, Jewish religious leaders were always asking him for a sign that he was the Messiah, the Son of God. Jesus refused and asked them just to have faith. After the resurrection, Thomas wanted proof that Jesus rose from the dead. He wanted the sign of wound prints in his actual body. Elton Trueblood explained what true faith is: "Faith is not belief without proof, but trust without reservation."

There are those who say, "It does not matter what you believe so long as you are sincere in that belief." Sincerity is no proof of true faith, for we can sincerely believe what is false. It is possible to be deadly in earnest and fully convinced that something is true, but it may be false. Sincerity in faith is a virtue only when the faith is genuine.

Then there is the false face of having faith in faith itself. Life demands faith for it to be satisfactory. We were made to have faith. Many of us feel like W. C. Fields, who said, "A man's got to believe in something. I believe I'll have another drink." Since faith is necessary for a satisfactory life, we have faith in faith, for faith results in health and happiness. For Christians faith does not always mean well-being and success. Faith may put us behind bars, in solitary confinement, or even on a cross.

One more false face of faith is the position that we should hold to our faith regardless of what that faith is. Some time ago a faithful Christian mother was upset when her son left the church for the Unification Church, the "Moonies." In commenting on her son's conversion to the sect, she said, "I think that if you believe in something, you have to stick to it." If we followed this type of thinking, we would always believe evil is good and Satan is god.

Triple-A Faith

You may belong to a Triple-A auto club, and as a Christian you have a Triple-A faith. When you are in a worship service and you say the Apostles' Creed, do you realize what you are saying when you say the word "believe"? Do you really mean it? If you knew the full meaning of "believe," would you still be willing to say it? This brings us to an understanding of the nature of faith. Belief has a Triple-A dimension — a spiritual AAA.

1. A — Assent

The first "A" is assent. This is an intellectual admission that a certain person or thing exists. It is like a child's believing that there is a Santa Claus. This is the easiest part of faith. It is an admission which does not require any responsibility for what you believe. To say "Jesus died" is just history. It does not have anything to do with me personally. According to a Gallup poll, 98 percent of the American people claim they believe in God. This is really not saying anything, for even Satan believes in the existence of God. This type of faith is a matter only of the mind; it is intellectual assent. It is expressed in the phrase, "I believe *that*...." The Apostles' Creed does not say "that." One day the French skeptic, Voltaire, went for a walk with a friend, and a procession came by. A man carrying a large cross led the procession. When the crucifix came by, Voltaire took off his hat as a respectful gesture. "What is this, Voltaire? Have you found God?" "No," replied Voltaire, "God and I salute, but we do not speak."

However, faith as assent is important because it gives content to our faith. What or whom do we believe? We may believe falsehood. We may have faith just in ourselves. Soon after being released from prison for his part in the Watergate scandal, G. Gordon Liddy boasted, "I found within myself all I need and all I shall ever need. I am a man of great faith, but my faith is in Gordon Liddy. I have never failed me."

Having faith in wrong ideas plagued the church through the centuries. If one believes that Jesus was only human, John cries, "Who is a liar but he who denies that Jesus is not of God?" (1 John 2:22). Not to believe in Jesus' resurrection means death: "If Christ has not been raised, your faith is futile and you are still in your sins" (1 Corinthians 15:17).

What then shall we believe? We believe in giving assent to the truths that God is our creating Father, that Jesus is the Christ, and that the Holy Spirit is God the comforter. When we say, "I believe," we are accepting the truths contained in the Apostles' Creed. This is *what* Christians believe.

2. A — Attitude

It is not enough to believe only in terms of assent. Faith goes beyond intellectual belief to the attitude of truth. In the creed we do not confess, "I believe *that*," but rather "I believe *in*...." There is a world of difference between "that" and "in." "That" refers to content, but "in" refers to trust in a person. There is a difference in saying "I believe you are a human" and "I believe in you." To believe in you means I put my trust in you, that you are a good and kind person. Christians say they believe in God, because our religion is a relationship with God based on trust in him.

The difference between assent and attitude of trust was illustrated by Blondin, a Frenchman who thrilled a large crowd by walking across Niagara Falls on a tightrope. When he got to the other side, he asked a spectator, "Do you believe I can carry a man across the falls?" The fellow replied, "Yes." "Do you believe that I can carry *you* across the falls?" At once the reply was "NO." The difference is when we say, "I believe Christ died." That is assent. When we say, "I believe Christ died for me," that is trust. With assent we use the mind. With trust we believe with the heart. Luther explained faith as trust:

> *To have a God properly means to have something in which the heart trusts completely. To have God, you see, does not mean to lay hands upon him, or put him in a purse, or shut him up in a chest. We lay hold on him when our heart embraces him and clings to him. To cling to him with our heart is nothing else than to entrust ourselves to him completely.*

If faith is an attitude of trust, in what or in whom do we trust? Do Americans trust in God, as our coins say? A Christian has the faith that trusts in God's Word with its promises. For instance, a Christian never walks alone, because he/she trusts in God's Word, "Lo, I am with you always" (Matthew 28:20). When we die, we relax in confidence because of the promise, "I will come again and take you to myself" (John 14:3). On the basis of our trust in God's Word, we know we are forgiven: "If we confess our sins, he will forgive our sins" (1 John 1:9). Some years ago I learned what it means to trust someone's word. My wife, Barbara, and I bought a condo in western North Carolina. The switch in the dining room had only an off-on switch. I suggested putting in a rheostat so that it might be more romantic for dinner by being able to reduce the light. She agreed and I went out and bought a rheostat. I decided to install it by myself. As I took off the plate of the switch, I suggested that I ought to go to the basement and turn off the main switch lest I get electrocuted. She said she would do it for me. I waited and waited but no word came from her whether she did it or not. I thought of going down to see if she turned it off, but then I thought she might see me and think I did not trust her word. So I said, "Here goes, God!" I touched the wires with my screwdriver. Because she was faithful to her word, I am here to show you I am alive!

We trust not only the promises and Word of God, but we trust our very lives to God by surrender and commitment. We commit our lives to him in utter trust that he knows best what we do with our lives. We rely upon him to lead and guide us through life. Some years ago I took up water-skiing. The first time I was able to get up on the skis, the boat pulled me to the center of a large lake. Losing confidence, I fell off the skis and the boat driver kept on going because he was not aware that I had fallen. Since I am a poor swimmer, I knew I could never swim to shore. There I was in the middle of a lake as helpless as anyone could be. Then I remembered I had on a ski belt. I decided to relax and wait for the boat to return. While waiting, I put my whole weight on the ski belt, trusted it to keep me from sinking, and enjoyed the wait. That is what faith is. We put our trust, our whole trust, on the everlasting arms of God.

3. A — Action

Action is the third "A" of faith. Faith is more than assent and attitude. However, many Christians stop in faith when it comes to doing something about their faith. James reminds us that faith without works is dead. When on a trip to England, we went to London and visited John Wesley's chapel. In back of the altar was a beautiful mahogany reredos of three parts. On the central panel Wesley had painted in gold lettering the Apostles' Creed. On the left panel was printed the greatest commandment, "Thou shalt love the Lord thy God...." On the right panel was the second greatest, "Thou shalt love thy neighbor as thyself." As Wesley's people worshiped Sunday after Sunday, they were reminded that the faith expressed in the creed must be expressed in obedience to the commandments.

True Christian faith calls for action. Faith works through action, the good works of love. Luther, who emphasized that we are saved by grace through faith, defined faith as follows:

> *It is a living, busy, active, mighty thing, this faith; and so it is impossible for it not to do good works incessantly. It does not ask whether there are good works to do, but before the question arises, it has already done them, and is always at the doing of them.*

It is a fact of life that we do what we believe in. Faith precedes action. Because Columbus believed that the world was round, he set sail for India by going west. Because the Nazis believed Jews were a menace to society, there was a holocaust. If we believe life begins at conception, we will be anti-abortionists. If we believe stocks are the best investment, we will buy stocks. If parents believe their children should have a college education, they will start saving from the time the child is born. If we believe that Jesus is the Christ, we will get baptized and join the church.

Faith calls for action in terms of obedience. The author of Hebrews writes, "By faith Abraham obeyed when he was called to go out to a place ... and he went out, not knowing where he was to go" (Hebrews 11:8). It was faith that made Isaiah say to God, "Here am I. Send me" (Isaiah 6:8). In his book, *Event in Eternity*, Paul Scherer wrote: "You just cannot hold on to your faith and expect anything much to happen. You cannot leave to others the doing of what really needs to be done. If this vision you have of God does not move and drive and pull and tug and wrench and twist and hold and stride and walk off grimly after him, it is nothing."

How can we say that we believe if we do not act on this faith? It is claimed that 98 percent of Americans believe in God. Do they really? What about the commandment, "Remember the sabbath day to keep it holy"? It means we are commanded to worship. Yet only thirty percent of church members are in church on a Sunday. The Bible teaches that the minimum gift God wants from us is a tenth of our income, but the average Christian donates only one percent. The average church today is a mission field!

60

How To Get Faith

When we consider the extreme importance of faith, we wonder how we can get it. Faith is too wonderful and difficult for it to be a human achievement. We are not born with faith. We cannot buy it. We are unable to earn or deserve it. Faith is not a matter of simple choice: "I think I'll believe." In contrast, as Luther said, "Faith is a divine work in us." The father of the epileptic boy at the foot of Mount Transfiguration asked Jesus to help him get more faith when he said, "I believe; help my unbelief" (Mark 9:22-24).

Faith is the divine work of the Holy Spirit. One of the nine fruits of the Spirit is faith. Paul taught, "to another faith by the same Spirit" (1 Corinthians 12:9). Again he wrote, "No one can say 'Jesus is Lord' except by the Holy Spirit" (1 Corinthians 12:3). One way the Spirit comes to us is in the hearing of God's Word. In Romans 10:17 Paul instructs us, "So faith comes from what is heard, and what is heard comes by the preaching of Christ." How does the hearing of the gospel produce faith? The Word brings with it the Spirit who creates faith in us. The Word (scripture) and Spirit are inseparable. The Word comes to us in sermon and sacrament as the oral and visible Word of God. This is one good reason for going to church — to get faith through the Spirit in the Word.

Now that we know what is involved when we say "I believe" in the creed, we realize more than ever that we need to say to Jesus, "Help my unbelief." We need divine help because faith embraces the whole person. It takes in the mind in terms of assent. It embraces the heart in terms of the attitude of trust. It involves the hand or whole body in terms of action. In your mercy, O Lord, hear our prayer: Increase our faith.

I Believe

Personal Experiences

1. Who went from hearing to seeing God? Read Job 42:5.
   Job

2. Who said, "My Lord and my God"? Read John 20:28.
   Thomas

3. Whose gospel did Paul preach? Read Romans 2:16.
   Paul

4. Tell about your personal experience:
   When did you first say, "I believe"? *1st remember w/ mrs. closer*
   What brought you to the point of saying, "I believe"?
   Did you understand what you were saying when you con-
   fessed, "I believe"?

The Importance Of Faith

What would be the consequence of having no faith? Find the
answers in the Bible references:
1. No faith: Not *saved*. See Acts 16:31.
2. No faith: No *miracles*. See Matthew 13:58.
3. No faith: No *power*. See Matthew 17:20.
4. No faith: No *life*. See John 11:25.
5. No faith: No _____. See James 2:22.

Source Of Faith

In the following passages, discover the answers by filling in the
blanks.
1. According to Matthew 3:7-9, faith cannot be *inherited*.
2. According to Acts 8:18-20, faith cannot be *bought*.
3. According to Romans 10:17, faith cannot be *death to the. words of christ*
4. According to Galatians 5:22, faith is a _____.

False Faith

Which of the following statements about faith are true or false? Circle the appropriate letter.

T ~~F~~ 1. "Faith is believing what you know ain't so."

T F 2. "If my father says it is so, it's so, even if it ain't so."

T ~~F~~ 3. "Seeing is believing."

T ~~F~~ 4. "It doesn't matter what you believe, as long as you are sincere."

T ~~F~~ 5. "Have faith in faith, for a person has to believe something."

T ~~F~~ 6. "If you believe something, you have to stick to it."

True Faith

True faith consists of assent, attitude, and action. Try this matching game. Place on each line the number that fits.

1 — Assent
2 — Attitude
3 — Action

_2_ Faith of the heart	_3_ Obedience	_3_ I respond
_1_ Faith of the mind	_2_ Trust	_1_ I believe *that*
_3_ Faith of the hand	_1_ Agreement	_2_ I believe *in*

63

Chapter 5

God The Father

In the Apostles' Creed a Christian confesses, "I believe in God the Father Almighty." Many consider the idea of God to be a problem. This prompts them to ask various questions about God which may be considered simple by some. One day a writer-mother of a four-year-old girl stayed home to reach a deadline. The child was watching a cartoon on television. She asked, "Mommy, who made the cartoons?" Her mother happened to see the credit line, "Hanna-Barbera." "Who is Hanna-Barbera?" "Just some people," the mother explained. "Who made the people?" Yelling, the mother answered, "God made the people." "But, Mommy, who made God?" By this time her mother lost her patience and her temper and screamed, "Carrie, go play!" Shrugging her shoulders, the child sighed, "Gee whiz! Ask a simple question!"

We have some "simple" but profound questions to ask about God. Is there really a God? Where did God come from? What is God like? Can we know him? Where is God? If we go to philosophers, we get a variety of answers. Sartre speaks of the silence of God; Heidegger of the absence of God; Jaspers of the concealment of God; Bultmann of the hiddenness of God; Buber of the eclipse of God; Tillich of the nonbeing of God; Altizer of the death of God. In contrast, the creed speaks of the almighty fatherhood of God.

The Making Of A God

The first simple question is, "What makes a god?" If 98 percent of the American people believe in the existence of God, do all these people believe in the one, true, and only God? Many believe in a god of their own making, but not in the one true God. When Moses was on the top of Mount Sinai for forty days, the people thought he and God had deserted them. They came to Aaron, the high priest, and demanded, "Up, make us gods" (Exodus 32:1).

Martin Luther gives the best definition of a god:

> *A god is that on which one should rely for everything good, and with which one can take refuge in every need. Thus to have a god is nothing other than to trust and believe in him from the heart — or, as I have often said, that only trust and faith in the heart make both God and a false god. If your faith and trust is right, then your God is right as well, and again where the belief is false and wrong, then the right God is absent, too. For the two belong together, faith and God. So that to which you give up and hand over your heart is truly your God.*

In summary, then, Luther tells us what makes a god: "Whatever, then, your heart clings to or relies upon, that, I say, is properly your God." In other words, your God is whatever or whoever comes first in your life. Accordingly, God is the top priority, the first principle, the *summum bonum*, and the ultimate concern of your life. Who really is number one in your life? You may say, "I believe in God," but your true God may not be the God of the scriptures.

Whatever or whoever comes first in your life is your god. For many the self is god as it is expressed in pride, egotism, arrogance, and self-centeredness. One cold night Vince Lombardi and his wife went to bed. When he came to bed, she screamed, "God, your feet are cold!" Vince replied, "Honey, you can call me Vince!" Various sects appeal to some by claiming that their followers are gods. The New Age tells us that to find God, we need just look in ourselves. Mormons are assured that if believers are faithful, they will eventually become gods.

Money is another popular god in our time. Money is so important that people will do anything to get it. In a recent book, *The Day America Told the Truth*, we are informed what some are willing to do for a million dollars: 25 percent would abandon their families, 20 percent would become prostitutes, 16 percent would renounce their American citizenship; and 7 percent would be willing to kill a stranger for a million dollars. Love of money is the root of all evil such as gambling, lottery, bribes, and drugs.

Sex is the god of many. According to *U.S. News and World Report* 80 percent of American women and 90 percent of men engage in premarital sex. One of every four children is born to an unwed mother. One and a half million women are raped annually. Seven billion dollars a year is spent on pornography. Prostitution, incest, and child molestation are common. This god of sex is ruining the lives of millions.

So, choose your own god! It is what you consider to be the most valuable thing or person in your life. If your god is one other than the true God, you are an idolater. When you say in the creed, "I believe in God," are you referring to the Father of our Lord Jesus or a god of your own making?

Does God Exist?

Another "simple" question: Does God exist? Can anyone prove the existence of God? According to the Apostles' Creed, the existence of God depends entirely upon faith: "I believe in God."

Various proofs have been offered over the ages that God does exist. There is the cosmological argument which is based upon nature. In nature we see beauty, design, and order. The beauty and power of the physical world cause us to conclude that behind the universe is a universe-maker just as there is a watchmaker behind a watch. It is not reasonable to say the universe just happened this way or that creation was an accident.

Another argument for the existence of God is the teleological one. In the universe we see that everything has a purpose. We call it ecology, the proper balance of nature. Disturb one part of nature and another part suffers. The plants, for example, produce oxygen for animals and people, and animals and people discharge carbon dioxide for food for plants. Each and every thing has a purpose. Behind the purpose in creation, we see a purpose in a Creator.

A third argument is known as the ontological one. It is the argument of an idea. If, the argument goes, humanity did not universally have the idea of God, there would be no God. In every person, there is an idea, a feeling, a longing for God. Because of this innate idea of a Being, the Being must exist.

Then there is the moral argument. In every human being there is a moral faculty. Each person has a conscience. It is a moral faculty that distinguishes between right and wrong. People of all ages and of all stages of development have a code of ethics. Instinctively they have standards of right and wrong. Where does humanity get this moral faculty? The answer is God.

Perhaps the most effective argument for the existence of God is the experiential one. This says that God is a reality because of one's experience with a Supreme Being. From prehistoric times, human beings have sought and responded to a god. Religion has always been the hub of life's wheel. Paintings, sculpture, music, prayers, and sacred writings testify to a universal belief in a god. Humanity is incurably religious and every people from the dawn of time has had some form of a god. This is due to the fact that man, male and female, was made a soul clothed in a body but in the image of God. The human is a spiritual being, and as Saint Augustine wrote, "We are restless until our souls rest in God."

For many these proofs are convincing that God exists. But the truth is that God's existence cannot be proved. There really are no proofs of the existence of God, there are only witnesses to his existence. As we have seen, God's existence depends ultimately on faith. Immanuel Kant in his *Critique of Pure Reason* put an end to human efforts to prove God's existence rationally. He pointed out that the natural cannot enter the supernatural area. The physical cannot prove the spiritual. As physical, rational beings we can go just as far as our minds and senses allow. The senses deal only with the world's phenomena. God and spirituality are in the world of the noumena, the spiritual arena.

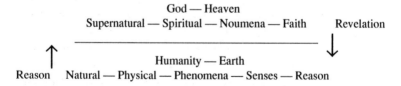

Because the natural with reason and senses must stop at the supernatural region of spirit, there is no way to prove God's existence. Only faith makes God a reality. There is no need then to try to argue religion or prove that God is a reality. For the unbeliever God will become a fact when the unbeliever accepts God by faith.

Can we know anything about God? As humans we can never find God, nor discover the truth of God by our reason, logic, observation, or experimentation. God is ultimately invisible and incomprehensible. What we know about God comes only by revelation. He reveals himself to us primarily in his Word. Through nature he reveals his power and majesty. In the mighty acts of history, he reveals himself as a divine deliverer of his people. His final and perfect disclosure is in his Son, Jesus. He shows us the Father, and all we need to know about God is in Jesus. He is God's final word of truth and grace. This revelation of God can be found in the scriptures. For evangelical Christians the Bible is the sole authority in matters of faith and life. No other book than the Bible can claim a greater knowledge of God, because the heart of the Bible is Christ who is the final revelation of God. Christians then are a people of one book.

You Are What You Believe

What you believe determines what you are and what you are NOT. You show your colors when you say, "I believe in God."

If you say that much of the creed, you are telling God, the church, and the world what you are NOT. You are not an atheist, one who denies the existence of God. At once we think of the famous atheist, Madalyn Murray O'Hair. The Bible responds, "The fool says in his heart, 'There is no God' " (Psalm 14:1).

Moreover, you are saying that you are NOT an agnostic, one who is not willing to deny or affirm the existence of God. The agnostic takes a middle path and will not say yes or no to God. The agnostic does not know whether God is or is not. The Bible says to the agnostic: "Because you are lukewarm, and neither cold nor hot, I will spew you out of my mouth" (Revelation 3:16).

If you say you believe in God, you are NOT a polytheist who believes that many gods exist. In New Testament times it is reported that more than 30,000 gods existed. Hindus are supposed to

69

have tens of thousands of gods. Anything or anyone can be made a god and worshiped, such as one's ancestors.

And you are NOT a henotheist. This is the view that there are many gods but one god is chief over the others. The Greeks had Zeus as chief god and the Romans had Jupiter. In Moses' day, according to the first commandment, Yahweh was the chief god for the Israelites. "You shall have no other gods before me."

And a pantheist you are NOT! "Pan" means "all." This view says that everything is God. The whole of nature — trees, bugs, birds, fish, snakes, people — is God. Creation and Creator are one and the same. Today we hear people say, "God is in nature." No, God is not in nature. God made nature. It is his handiwork. A shoe is the work of a shoemaker, but the shoe is not the shoemaker. In the same way, the physical world is not God. There is no sense in worshiping the sun, moon, or stars.

When you say, "I believe in God," you are saying you are NOT a deist. This view holds that though God exists, he is not concerned about the world and is not involved in it. Deists claim that God made the world, established the laws of nature, and then went back to heaven and let the world run itself according to the laws. He does not care what happens to the world, nor does he get involved with people. If the world runs by laws, there is no place for prayer or miracles. Some of our famous American statesmen in the colonial period were deists: Benjamin Franklin and Thomas Jefferson.

If we are not any of these, what are we when we say, "I believe in God"? By that statement you indicate that you are not only a theist but also a monotheist. A theist is one who believes in God and a monotheist believes in only one God. In the creed we say we believe in God *the* Father, not "a" Father. This is to say that there is no other real God in existence. All other gods are the product of human minds and imagination. These gods have no real or objective existence. They cannot because God created everything there is and he did not create other gods. This gives the church reason to send missionaries to lands where they do not know of the one and only God. Lay people in America need to hear this, too. In a poll of lay church people, 42 percent agreed with the statement, "Of many

70

.

religions in the world, most lead to God." The Bible is clear about this: "The Lord our God is one Lord" (Deuteronomy 6:4). Paul witnesses: "One Lord, one faith, one baptism, one God and Father of us all, who is above all and through all and in all" (Ephesians 4:5-6).

What Is God Like?

"What is God like?" is our next "simple" question. The creed answers, "I believe in God the Father Almighty." Of the very many attributes we could give God, the creed gives us only two: "father" and "almighty." These are the two basic characteristics of the nature of God. They give us two understandings of God and two systems of thought about God. The following list may help us to understand; explanations will follow.

God

Subject	God the Father	God the Almighty King
1. Nature of God	Love	Justice
2. Domain of God	Immanence	Transcendence
3. Being of God	Person (Willing to save)	Power (Able to save)
4. Nature of the human	Child of the Father	Subject of the Kingdom
5. Method	Free choice (of the human)	Election (by God)
6. Freedom	Foreknowledge	Predestination
7. Ethics	Conscience	Laws
8. Motivation	Gratitude	Fear
9. Result	Salvation	Judgment
10. Word of God	Gospel	Law

An explanation may be helpful to understand this list:

1. Nature of God: Love and Justice

Jesus referred to God as Father 170 times. As a father, God loves his children. In fact, the Bible tells us that God is love (1 John 4:8). But God is more than love. He is justice. This implies the holiness of God dealing with righteousness. It involves the wrath of God against sin and ultimately judgment.

2. Domain of God: Immanence and Transcendence

Where is God? Is he available and approachable or is he too distant for us to reach him? The concept of Father speaks of God's immanence. He is a God with us and for us. He is nearer than

71

hands and closer than breathing. He is approachable and always ready-at-hand. In recent years immanence was symbolically portrayed by bringing the altar from the east wall down close to the pews. The altar became freestanding so that the minister at the altar would face the congregation during worship. "Almighty" gives the other side of God — his transcendence. This means that God is the totally other from the human. He is hidden and unknowable. He is the God of glory, power, and majesty. This makes us stand in awe and adoration and we sing "How Great Thou Art."

The difference between immanence and transcendence can be seen in the story about the meeting of former President Reagan and former Israeli Prime Minister Begin in the White House. In Reagan's oval office there were three telephones: a white one for local calls, a red one for the hot line to Russia, and a gold one to God. He asked Begin if he wanted to speak to God. Begin did and after the call he asked about the long distance charge. It was ten dollars. Some time later Reagan visited Begin in his office where there were again three phones. Begin asked Reagan whether he wanted to speak to God. When Reagan finished, he asked about the charges. Begin said there were no charges because it was a local call! The difference between immanence and transcendence is the difference between a local and long distance call.

3. **Being of God: Person and Power**

The concept of "Father" means that God is a person or personality. He is not a person in the sense that he is manlike. This could lead to an anthropomorphic concept of God as a white-haired godfather in the skies. God was not made in the image of man but man was made in the image of God. Man is like God in that the human is essentially a spiritual being (a soul) clothed in a physical body. As a person God is one who knows, feels, and wills. As a person God is one who hates evil, loves the good, gets angry at disobedience, and remembers the plight of his children. As a person God is always willing to save and to help.

God as "Almighty" indicates he is power. The Bible asks, "Is there anything too hard for God?" and answers, "With God all things are possible." As Father God is willing to help us; as Almighty he is able to help us. God's power is seen in his ability to transform evil into good, to bring life out of death, and to create something out of nothing.

4. Nature of the human: Child of the Father and Subject of the Kingdom

Since God is our Father, then who are we? A father has children, and we are children of the heavenly Father by virtue of our baptism. As children we can cheerfully and confidently come into his presence. As Father, God gives only good things to his children. Jesus asked, "If a child asks for bread, will his father give him a stone?" As children, our relationship with God the Father is one of warmth and intimacy.

Our Almighty God has power like unto a king. No one has greater power than a king. In fact, God in Christ is King of kings and Lord of lords. He has all power and authority. This makes us subjects of the King and servants in his kingdom. As subjects, we are under his protection and care. In turn, we are expected to be loyal and obedient servants.

5. Method: Free choice and Election

How does one become a child or subject of God? Does a person have a choice? Or do we have nothing to do about it? In the Father relationship, we are children of God because we freely responded to God. When he said through his Son, "Come to me," we can choose to come or not to come. The Spirit draws us, seeks us, wants us, but by our wills we can reject the promptings of the Spirit. If we do that, Jesus said we commit the unpardonable sin.

On the other hand, God as sovereign King chooses us by election. He decides who will be in his Kingdom. We are called and elected to salvation or to judgment, to heaven or hell. The Bible tells us that God calls us to be his people. Paul writes that God destines us to be saved. We are a chosen people.

6. Freedom: Foreknowledge and Predestination

God the Father knows all things and knows what will happen before it happens. This is called foreknowledge. God knew humanity would fall into sin. Therefore, from the foundation of the world, he devised a plan to save it by sending a Savior. Predestination fits into the concept of God as "Almighty." Since he is the almighty king, he orders all things, and nothing occurs contrary to his will. In foreknowledge God knows what will happen but does not necessarily make it happen. In predestination there is no freedom of choice. It is as God wills it. This can lead to fatalism. Not all things happen because they are God's will.

The difference between foreknowledge and predestination is illustrated in the case of two ministers who decided to exchange pulpits one Sunday. On the way to the churches, they passed each other. The one said, "My good friend, is it not wonderful to contemplate that before the world was created, it was decided in the councils of heaven that, on this particular day, you would preach in my church and I in yours?" The other replied, "In that case, I won't do it!" He turned around and went back to his own church. God had the foreknowledge that the preacher was going to change his mind. The other preacher probably held that the change of mind was predestined.

7. Ethics: Conscience and Laws

How are we to live our lives? What will motivate us to love and serve God? What are the standards? Are there any limits to our behavior? When we accept God as Father, we know we are his children by grace. Christ has freed us from the demands of the Law by fulfilling the Law for us. Are we then against the Law and free to break it? By no means! Instead of being slaves to the Law, God has given us a moral faculty called the conscience. This conscience is enlightened by the Holy Spirit. So in freedom we live by our consciences. With the concept of God as sovereign King, he rules by the laws of the Kingdom and he demands we obey his laws or else! This can lead to legalism for the average person. Life becomes a series of "Do this" or "Don't do that."

8. Motivation: Gratitude and Fear

Why should we be good people? Why be honest and kind and loving? What is the reason for it? As Father, God is love and loves us. His love was demonstrated in the death of his Son for our salvation on a cruel cross. When we think of God's innumerable blessings, his gift of being made right with God, and his assurance that we will live with him forever, we are overcome with a deep sense of gratitude. "God, you have done so much for me; what can I do for you?"

When we think of the Almighty God as sovereign King full of justice and holiness, we obey his commandments out of fear. We are afraid to offend him. We behave because we fear the punishment. In his explanation of each of the Ten Commandments, Luther said, "We should so fear and love God...."

9. Result: Salvation and Judgment

Salvation comes from a loving God the Father. If we respond to his love with repentance and faith, God accepts us and forgives us. He saves us from death and hell. On the other hand, God as the Almighty King will come to the world for a final judgment. Wrongs must be righted. Unrepentant sinners must be punished. The King will separate the sheep from the goats when he returns for judgment.

10. Word of God: Gospel and Law

The Word of God consists of Gospel and Law. The Gospel can be seen in the list under "God the Father." Here we find mercy and salvation. Under God as Almighty King we find the Law. The Gospel is the good news that God loves us enough to let his Son die for us. The Word of God recorded in the Bible is composed of both Gospel and Law. Both are equally important and we need both. Without the Gospel, we would die in our sins. Without the Law, we would need no Gospel. Our task is to keep the two in proper balance. If a balance is not possible, then 51 percent should be Gospel.

God The Father

What is your answer?

1. Is there really a God?

2. What constitutes a god?

3. Can God's existence be proved?

4. What is this God like?

5. Are we to fear or love him or both?

6. Is God a "she," "he," or "it"?

What makes a God:

Check your answers:
1. ___ Whoever or whatever comes first in your life.
2. ___ Whatever you consider to be the greatest good.
3. ___ Whoever or whatever dominates your life.
4. ___ Whatever your heart clings to or relies upon.

A self-made God
1. ___ Self: "I am number one."
2. ___ Money: Do you agree with Ecclesiastes 10:19?
3. ___ Power: a dictator
4. ___ Sex: pornography, fornication, rape, abuse
5. ___ Race: Jews and Arabs
6. ___ Pleasure: "Eat, drink, for tomorrow we die." Read 1
Corinthians 15:32.

What kind of believer are you?
1. ___ Atheism: "I believe there is no God."
2. ___ Agnosticism: "I do not know whether or not God exists."
3. ___ Polytheism: "I believe in many gods."
4. ___ Pantheism: "I believe everything and everyone is God."
5. ___ Henotheism: "I believe God is the chief of gods."
6. ___ Deism: "I believe God created the world and left it to be run by laws."
7. ___ Monotheism: "I believe there is only one true God and all other gods are nonexistent."

If God is the only true God —
1. Do all religions lead to God?

2. Is one religion as good as another?

3. Is there any value or truth in non-Christian religions?

4. Are believers in non-Christian religions lost?

Chapter 6

God The Creator

A surgeon, an engineer, and a politician were arguing which profession was the oldest. "Eve was made from Adam's rib," said the surgeon, "and that, of course, was a surgical procedure." "Yes," countered the engineer, "but before that, order was created out of chaos, and that most certainly was an engineering job." "Ah-ha!" exclaimed the politician triumphantly. "And just who do you think created the chaos?" If a spokesman for God were present, he probably said, "You men know nothing. Before anyone or anything, God was there 'in the beginning.'" The creed speaks for the Bible when it has us say: "I believe in God the Father Almighty, maker of heaven and earth" or "I believe in God the Father Almighty, creator of heaven and earth."

The only difference between the traditional and ecumenical versions is in the words "maker" and "creator." The latter word has a greater significance than the former. God the Father is the creator of the universe, not only the "maker." Only God can create but almost everyone can make things. Creation requires that something be made out of nothing — *creator ex nihilo*. Before the creation, the earth was "without form and void, and darkness ..." (Genesis 1:2). People may be creative but not creators. We can rearrange things in different patterns, but we cannot create something out of nothing. That is why only God can make a Christian, for a Christian is a new creation (2 Corinthians 5:17). A Christian must first die to self and become nothing. Then he rises with Christ into a new creation. New life is created out of death, the death of the Old Adam. We must first become nothing before God can make something out of us.

Who Made The Universe?

Not everyone agrees with the creed that God is the creator. Scientists propose the big bang theory of the birth of the universe.

Astronomers have long believed that galaxies, clusters that usually contain billions of stars, were all formed shortly after the big bang which was the cataclysmic explosion some fifteen billion years ago that resulted in the universe. Others claim there was no creation because of the permanence of creation. This is supported by virtue of a continuous creation. This makes the universe eternal. New stars are continually being discovered. This view is known as "the steady state theory."

The creed expresses the faith that creation is the work of God the Father. He created both heaven and earth. This refers to the entire universe with all the planets and stars including the earth and all that is on it. While God the Father is given credit for creation, the other persons of the Trinity were with the Father as participants in the creation. God the Son shared in creation: "All things were made through him, and without him was not anything made that was made" (John 1:3). God the Spirit also had a part in creation: "The Spirit of God was moving over the face of the waters" (Genesis 1:2).

Creation was something only the triune God could do. To create an infinite universe, it took an infinite God. Think of the vastness of the universe. Today astronomers study stars so distant that their light, traveling at 186,000 miles per second, has been moving toward the earth for more than ten billion years. Or consider the age of the universe. Some astrophysicists claim that the universe is from fifteen to twenty billion years of age. For this to be created, there had to be a God who is "from everlasting to everlasting." Then think of the size of the universe. There are billions upon billions of stars, like our sun, that continually burn like thermonuclear furnaces.

Above all, there is the creation of humankind, the very crown of creation. The human being is a marvel of creation. The human body has thirty trillion cells performing 10,000 chemical functions. The body has 206 bones, 639 muscles, and a brain that processes 10,000 thoughts per day and communicates 4,000 messages. The heart beats over 100,000 times daily and pumps blood 168,000,000 miles around the body. Consider the human lungs. The average person takes 23,800 breaths per day to bring 438 cubic feet of air to the lungs.

In light of all this, we can see that only God could create the universe. "The heavens are telling the glory of God and the firmament proclaims his handiwork" (Psalm 19:1).

Continuing Creation

Creation is not only a thing of the past but it still goes on. The first verse of the Bible begins, "In the beginning *when* God created the heavens and the earth." The word "when" gives the impression that creation was a onetime event. But an alternate translation in the same version says, "When God *began* to create."

God's continuing creation is seen in our ever-expanding universe. Astronomers claim that the galaxies are ever-expanding. Stars are constantly being born and others are dying. It takes billions of years for some stars to die out.

Even the earth is in the process of creation. The planet earth is constantly renewing her surfaces and changing her face in vast movements of the crustal plates. New landforms are coming into existence. Internally the earth moves. This is seen in earthquakes and volcanoes. Scientists are of the opinion that our multi-billion-year-old earth is still evolving.

We can be grateful for continuing creation, because it provides the necessities of life. Through sun, rain, seasons, the power of life in seed, and the basic instinct of self-preservation, God continues his creation. We are ever-dependent on God to provide the necessities of life through nature. We live from hand-to-mouth similar to the Israelites in the wilderness who received manna on a day-to-day basis. We experience the providence of God through his continuous creation. The creation of God and the providence of God are two sides of a coin.

Implications

What does this truth about God's work of creation mean to us? Are there any implications for our lives today?

First, in the face of these facts about the universe, we are impressed with the greatness of God. In the face of an infinite universe, we see how great our God is. We appreciate the power of God which made the universe. A tornado, hurricane, or a thunderstorm helps us realize the almightiness of God. Thus, we come to the conclusion that there is nothing too hard for God to do for us when we ask for his help. He is able to keep his promises. Before his greatness and power, we instinctively bow in awe, reverence, and adoration.

Another implication of God as creator is our stewardship of the earth. This is not our world but God's world by virtue of his having made it. If he made it, he knows how to fix it, for surely our world is in need of fixing. Years ago a Ford car broke down on a highway. The owner did not know what was wrong with it, and if he did, he would not have known how to fix it. A fellow traveler stopped and offered his help. In a short time the stranger had the car running again. The owner asked, "How did you know how to fix it? Who are you?" The stranger explained, "I know how to fix it because I am the man that made it. You see, I am Henry Ford." In the same way, only God can repair our broken, ailing, out-of-commission world, because like none other, he understands and knows what is wrong. And what is wrong? It is the heart of every human being.

Since God is the owner and maker of the world, we humans are only trustees and stewards. God placed the care and dominance of nature into human hands. At the very beginning, "The Lord God took the man and put him in the garden of Eden to till it and keep it" (Genesis 2:15). God made us gardeners and caretakers of his creation. Tragically, many in our day have forgotten humanity's role in creation. We are squandering and wasting natural resources. We have ravished and polluted the good earth. Acid rain is bringing our lakes and forests to ruin. Many animals and birds are on the endangered species list. Through greed we are cutting down rain forests, and paving with asphalt fields that formerly were feeding and breeding grounds for birds and animals. Our insatiable demand for energy is exhausting natural resources. If Americans would go back to hanging out their clothes to dry, enough electricity would be saved to provide electricity for 3.2 million homes. Half of the natural gas used is due to the burning of pilot lights on our stoves.

It takes 800 acres of timber to produce the Sunday issue of *The New York Times*. In one state, seventeen percent of its solid waste materials is disposable diapers. All of these facts point to the need for conservation. One day God may ask us, "What have you done to my earth?"

A third implication is the value of human life. Human beings are the special creation of God, the crown of his entire creation. Our bodies are "fearfully and wonderfully made" (Psalm 139:14). This body of mine is really not mine. It is God's because he made it for my use. If the body belongs to God by virtue of creation, I cannot say that I can do with it as I please. I did not choose to be born. I did not make myself. Therefore, I am only a trustee of my body. I am responsible to God to care for the body, to keep it in good health as far as possible. I dare not waste my life by indulging in harmful foods or activities. Each year 350,000 lives are lost through smoking tobacco. If my life is not my own, I have no right to end it in suicide. Yet each year 50,000 youth commit this irreversible sin.

What is true about the body is also true about the soul. God has made us basically souls which are clothed with bodies. When Adam was created, his body was made first and then God breathed his Spirit into him and he became a "living being" (Genesis 2:7). Consequently, we are responsible for taking care of our souls also. They need spiritual food through private and public worship, Bible reading, and prayer. The danger is that we become so concerned about our physical well-being that we neglect our souls. With this in mind, Jesus asked, "What does it profit a man to gain the whole world and forfeit his life?" (Mark 8:36).

A fourth implication of God's creation is the power of God's Word. He created the universe by his Word. In the Genesis account, we read time after time, "And God said." When he spoke, order came out of chaos, light overcame the darkness, life came to animals and man. The power of God is in the power of his Word. Word and deed are one. The Word has power to heal and to transform life from evil to good. For this reason we need to read, learn, and digest God's Word.

Why Was The World Created?

The Apostles' Creed tells us *who* created the universe, but it does not tell us *why*. Nor does the Bible in chapter and verse tell us why. Yet the question is always bothering us. Did God have a reason for creating the world?

One answer is that God created the world for his own sake. The Bible tells us that God is love. If God is love, then he, like us, needs someone to love. Before humanity was created, a lonely God said, "Let us make humankind in our image, after our likeness" (Genesis 1:26). God needed a creature like himself whom he could love and who could love him. Birds, animals, and flowers are incapable of loving as humans do. If one loves and has no one to love in return, it is agony and utter frustration. It can be a tragedy of unrequited love. Humans were made out of love in order to love in return. Just as we need love, to love and to receive love, God needed creatures to love and for them to love him.

With this in mind, we can see a reason for our creation. We were made to love and to have fellowship with God. When we accept God's love and love him in return, we find meaning and fulfillment in life. When we are in love with God and not with self, life is abundant with peace and joy. When humanity fell out of love with God by disobeying him, sin, suffering, shame, and death came into human existence. Since Adam and Eve, humanity turned from God, resisted God, and became his enemy. Since that original sin, God has been seeking, yearning, and begging humanity to return to him, as he continues to love his people. It is the long, long story of God's plan of salvation. Through prophets, priests, kings, acts of history, and finally through his own Son, God reaches out to people and says, "Turn to me and live."

A second possible answer to why God created the heavens and the earth is that he created them for humanity's sake. The just-created human race had to have a garden for food, drink, and clothing. Just after the Fall, God makes clothes for Adam and Eve. The universe was made for humanity's welfare, for life and enjoyment. Consequently, everything God made was good. In the creation account, after each stage of creation, it is said that God looked at it and pronounced it good. "God saw that it was very good." The earth was created, moreover, for our good, because the whole creation is good. When mankind cares for the earth, each person enjoys the products of the earth. When humanity neglects, ravishes, exploits, abuses, and wastes the earth, it suffers. Some years ago a horrible famine with wholesale starvation was experienced in Africa. A drought was only a small part of the cause. The main reason for the famine was the cutting down of forests and the exploitation of the land to the point that there was little to no topsoil for growing food.

The biblical view of the physical world is that God's creation is good. Docetism and Gnosticism taught that matter was inherently evil. This was the view of many Puritans. The material world was supposed to be evil and associated with the devil. In contrast, the Bible teaches that the human body with all its functions, organs, and drives is inherently good. Call nothing that God made evil. A good God can only create good things. When the body's drives and desires are exploited, abused, and misused, evil and sin result. Sex is considered by some as dirty and bad. According to God's Word, sex is a gift of God for a couple's ability to have children and to promote a closer relationship between a husband and wife. Sex can be beautiful and honorable. It is when sex is used outside marriage, when it is polluted by fornication, incest, pornography, and harassment, that it becomes a curse to humankind.

The How Of Creation

The Apostles' Creed does not tell us when creation took place, how it was done, or how long it took to bring it to its present state. It does not tell us simply because the Bible is silent in these matters. As a result there is a difference of opinion. A Gallup poll in 1991 indicated that 47 percent of Americans believe God created humankind in his/her present form within the past 10,000 years. Forty percent believe humans developed over millions of years but God guided the process. Nine percent believe God was not involved in the process. Christians are divided on this issue: 49 percent of Protestants accept creationism; 55 percent of Roman Catholics go for evolution.

On the one hand, there is the very conservative explanation of creation known as creationism. Fundamentalist Christians, who take the Bible literally, word for word as dictated by God, hold to the position known as creationism. They maintain that the origin of the universe and life rests with God's actions as recorded in Genesis 1 and 2. Accordingly, they hold that the universe came into existence within the past 10,000 years. It took God only six 24-hour days to create the entire universe and everything on earth. God's method was instantaneous.

This view repudiates the scientific view of evolution which maintains that the diversity of life on earth is the outcome of evolution. Evolution is an unsupervised, impersonal, unpredictable, and natural process of temporal descent with genetic modification that is affected by natural selection, chance, historical contingencies, and changing environments. Creationists claim that the Bible is the God-inspired account of creation and is to be taken as it says.

These ultraconservative Christians insist that this biblical view should be taught in public schools in place of evolution. Thirty-one states have a law directing that if evolution is taught in public schools, creationism should also be taught. In 1987 the Supreme Court of the United States struck down a Louisiana law requiring the teaching of creationism where evolution is taught.

On the other hand, there is the modern scientific explanation of creation that says the earth is about 4.5 billion years old, in contrast to creationism's contention that the earth is no older than 10,000 years. Fossils and rocks are billions of years old. The diamond is the earth's oldest rock — 3.5 billion years old. Over the billions of years came fish, amphibians, plants, insects, reptiles, dinosaurs, birds, and mammals. Three-and-a-half million years ago came the walking primates that ended in modern man and woman.

There are two kinds of evolution. There is secular evolution which has no place for God in the process of creation. Everything, they say, came into existence from a "big bang," from various chemicals, and developed according to natural selection and reproduction. Evolution then has no connection with a Creator.

The other kind of evolution can be called theistic evolution. This view has a place for God who is the Cause of the evolutionary process. In this case, evolution does not deny divine creation but only describes it. It acknowledges that God is the maker of the universe and evolution is his way of bringing the universe to its present status. A little girl was watching a television program dealing with evolution. Her mother tried to interrupt and give a religious explanation of creation. The girl responded, "Be quiet, Mother. I want to learn how God did these things." You may ask, does this view not conflict with the Bible? There really is no conflict between science and religion. As someone said, "Science is about knowing. It's not about believing." It does not matter whether God took six days or six billion years to create the universe. The Bible does not pose as an authority in science, history, politics, or sociology. Its authority is in the realm of spiritual truth. When Galileo was on trial for his support of the Copernican view of the universe, he quoted a churchman of his day: "The intention of the Holy Spirit is to teach how to go to heaven and not how go the heavens." An Episcopal bishop said he did not know a single reputable biblical scholar who would say that God created man in the last 10,000 years. In 1985 Pope John Paul spoke to a group of scientists on evolution: "Belief in evolution is not blocked by faith, if discussion of it remains in the context of the naturalistic method and its possibilities. The biblical account of creation and belief in God are not incompatible with the theory of evolution."

A study of Genesis 1 shows how the world evolved. In verse 2 there is total darkness. Light overcomes the darkness in verse 3. Water then comes in verse 6. After the water, land appears as the water recedes — verse 9. With the land in place, vegetation comes — verse 12. Later come fish and birds — verse 20. In verse 24 we have the animals. To top it all, human beings come as the last and crown of the entire creation — verse 26.

Where Do You Stand?

You can confess the Apostles' Creed without entering into the creation-creationism controversy, because the creed tells us only who created the universe and not how or how long it took for creation. You can be a true Christian whether you are a creationist or an evolutionist. It is a matter of personal choice between two explanations. You may prefer Moses' pre-scientific explanation or the modern scientific view. The essential for both parties is the acceptance of the creed's truth: God is the creator of the heavens and earth. How God did it or how long it took for him to do it is nonessential.

A Summary Of The First Article Of The Apostles' Creed

This You Can Believe

I believe that God has created me and all that exists; that he has given and still preserves to me my body and soul, with all my limbs and senses, my reason and all the faculties of my mind, together with my raiment, food, home, and family, and all my property; that he daily provides me abundantly with all the necessities of life, protects me from all danger, and preserves me and guards me against all evil; all which he does out of pure, paternal, and divine goodness and mercy, without any merit or worthiness in me; for all which I am in duty bound to thank, praise, serve, and obey him. This is most certainly true.

— Martin Luther, *The Small Catechism*

God The Creator

The Apostles' Creed answers some of our questions about the creation of the universe, but not all of them. What questions are answered or not answered?

Answered Questions
WHO created the universe?

The creed answers: GOD. Science answers: BIG BANG. Which is correct?

If God did it, was it God the Father only? Where were God the Son and God the Holy Spirit? For the answers read:

Genesis 1:1 _____

John 1:3 _____

Genesis 1:2 _____

WHAT was created?

The creed says God created heaven and earth. What do you understand by "heaven"? Is it the place we faithful Christians go when we die? Does "earth" include insects, rats, mosquitoes, dragons, dinosaurs, snakes, the devil?

Do all God's creatures have a right to live? What about the endangered species? Can we undo what God has done? Is a Christian a natural conservationist?

WHEN was the universe created?

Fundamentalists say creation took place less than 10,000 years ago. Modern scientists claim the universe began ten billion years ago. The Bible says, "In the beginning God created ..." (Genesis 1:1). The key is knowing when was the "beginning." Do rocks and fossils give us a clue to how old the earth is? The Bible is right: the universe had to have a beginning. If it were eternal, then the universe would be God who is eternal.

Unanswered Questions
WHY did God create the heavens and earth?

The creed does not tell us why. We can get a glimpse of the "why" in the Bible. From your knowledge of the Bible, why do you think God made the universe? Check the following that you agree with:

____ To have someone for God to love.

____ To provide a place for humanity to live.

____ To give people the joy of seeing creation.

____ To permit people to experience life.

____ To test the loyalty of his children.

____ To create for the sake of creating.

HOW and HOW LONG?

What method did God use to create the world? How long did it take him to do it? Discuss with those around you the following questions:

1. Does it really matter if God took six days or six billion years to complete his creation?

2. Is the Genesis account a religious or scientific explanation of creation?

3. If one chooses the evolution theory, is one unfaithful to the Bible?

4. Is the biblical account of creation to be taken literally?

5. Can one be a true Christian and accept evolution?

6. Is the Bible an authority in science?

7. Should creationism be taught in our public schools?

God The Son

The Second Article Of The Apostles' Creed

Traditional Version

"And in Jesus Christ, his only Son our Lord, who was conceived by the Holy Ghost, born of the Virgin Mary, suffered under Pontius Pilate, was crucified, dead, and buried. He descended into hell; the third day he rose again from the dead; he ascended into heaven, and sitteth on the right hand of God the Father Almighty; from thence he shall come to judge the quick and the dead."

Ecumenical Version

"I believe in Jesus Christ, his only Son, our Lord. He was conceived by the power of the Holy Spirit and born of the virgin Mary. He suffered under Pontius Pilate, was crucified, died, and was buried. He descended to the dead. On the third day he rose again. He ascended into heaven, and is seated at the right hand of the Father. He will come again to judge the living and the dead."

Chapter 7

The Human Jesus

Who is Jesus? This is the most popular question in the church as well as in the world during the 1990s. In 1996 three top secular magazines in America, *Time, Newsweek*, and *U.S. News and World Report*, carried feature articles on the subject of Jesus and had a portrait of him on the front cover. The three main television networks, ABC, CBS, and NBC, featured the question on their news programs. Dozens of books have been written on the subject. Jesus is the primary discussion topic among New Testament scholars, theologians, and churchmen. The average church member is distressed and shocked at what is said and written about Jesus.

What is the cause of this turmoil? It is largely due to the Jesus Seminar, an association of 75 New Testament scholars led by John Dominic Crossan and Robert Funk. These scholars claim that the four Gospels are fiction resulting from the authors' creative imagination. Eighty-two percent of Jesus' words are held to be inauthentic. Accordingly, we cannot be sure of anything Jesus said. Rudolf Bultmann, top New Testament scholar of the twentieth century, wrote, "We can now know almost nothing concerning the life and personality of Jesus." The subject of Jesus is divided into the Jesus of history and the Christ of faith, the pre-Easter Jesus and the post-Easter Christ. The Jesus of history is not real. The Incarnation, Virgin Birth, Resurrection, and Ascension as well as the miracles are denied as historical facts.

Now, more than ever, we need to face the question, "Who is the real Jesus?" Is the Christ of faith the Jesus of history? What is the truth about Jesus? What can we believe? We turn to the Apostles' Creed which has given the church's answer for 2,000 years.

Different Positions

It is not strange that the most popular question of our time is, "Who is Jesus?" Was this question not answered in Matthew 16:16

93

when Peter said to Jesus at Caesarea Philippi: "You are the Messiah, the Son of the living God"? In Jesus' day, too, there were different opinions about Jesus. When on a retreat with his disciples, he asked them what people were saying about him. The public was divided: Jesus was considered to be John the Baptist, Elijah, Jeremiah, or one of the prophets. What more of an answer do we need than the answer of Peter? Jesus accepted his answer as the truth, for he said, "Blessed are you, Simon, son of Jonah! For flesh and blood has not revealed this to you, but my Father in heaven" (Matthew 16:17). Yet, after twenty centuries, we do not believe what Peter said about the identity of Jesus. According to a Gallup poll, 42 percent of Americans agreed with the statement: "Jesus is the Son of God." A recent report from Germany indicated that only one out of every four believe in Jesus Christ. Throughout Christian history down to the present, there are different views of Jesus. Now let us look at some of them.

1. The All-Human Jesus

According to this position, Jesus is 100 percent human. It was held as early as the first centuries of Christianity by the Ebionites. They denied that Jesus was divine. He was only a teacher, prophet, miracle-man, and one with an outstanding character. But he was not divine, the Son of God. Today this view is held by many, including atheists, agnostics, Unitarians, Jews, Moslems, and other non-Christian religions.

2. The All-Divine Jesus

Opposite the Ebionites, Docetists held that Jesus was entirely divine. He was not at all human. This view was originally taught by Eutychus, a monk in a monastery near Constantinople. In the fourth century, Appolonarius, bishop of Laodicea, popularized the teaching. It was known as Docetism, from the Latin word *docere* meaning "to seem." It just seemed that Jesus was human. It was based on the idea that the physical and material were inherently evil. The human body therefore was sinful. Jesus therefore was not human, for God could not be identified with sin. Docetists held that Jesus' human nature was swallowed up by the divine. This denied the Incarnation, the biblical teaching that "the Word became flesh."

3. The Half And Half Jesus

Nestorians took the view that Jesus was half human and half divine. It was taught by Nestorius, bishop of Constantinople, in the fifth century. To this day it is a very popular understanding of Jesus. When we see Jesus hungry, thirsty, and tired, we say it was because he was human. When he struggles in prayer and on the cross cries out, "My God, why ...?" we see the human Jesus. On the other hand, Jesus is God when he walks on water, feeds 5,000, raises the dead, heals lepers, and rises from the grave. The problem with this view is that we have a divided Jesus — two persons in one body.

4. The Adopted Jesus

This is known as adoptionism. According to this position, Jesus came into the world as a human. Because of his moral excellence, his perfect obedience to God, his wisdom, his compassion for people, and his willing sacrifice of himself on the cross, the Father adopted him as his son at his baptism. This adoption was confirmed by the resurrection and the ascension. Jesus then became a deified man.

5. **The Both/And Jesus**

The above different positions concerning Jesus caused great concern, for the gospel was at stake. If Jesus were only human, then he was just a martyr on the cross and not the Lamb that took away the sin of the world. If he were only human, the resurrection was a fairy tale. His promises of forgiveness and eternal life were meaningless. His claims to know God and to be one with God would then be the words of a religious fanatic who was deluded into thinking he was the Son of God.

On the other hand, if Jesus were only divine and not human, humanity would be the loser. Because he was human, he became one of us. As a human, he fulfilled the law for us. Through his humanity we could see the nature of God. Above all, he became sin for us so that sin, through him, could go out of the world. As a human Jesus knows our human condition. Like all of us he was tempted and he showed that by the power of God we can overcome temptation to sin.

Consequently, the church had to take a stand on the question of Jesus. Is he only human, only divine, or half and half? In 451 A.D. the church held a council at Chalcedon to decide the issue. The church decided that it was not a matter of Jesus being fully God or fully human, or half and half, but it was a matter of both,

both fully human *and* fully divine. To this day the church holds to this truth stated at Chalcedon:

> *We confess one and the same Son, our Lord Jesus Christ, perfect in manhood, truly God and truly man, or a rational soul and a body, of one substance with the Father with respect to the Godhead, and of one substance with us in respect of the manhood, like us in everything but sin ...*

This is to say that Jesus is fully God and fully man. These two natures are blended into one integrated personality. He is not a split personality, nor does he suffer from schizophrenia. It is like a blender in your kitchen. Suppose you put apples, peaches, and pears in it and pushed the "on" button for a minute. Now what do you have — apples, peaches, and pears? Yes, you do, but can you tell which is which? They have become one fruit, one substance. Also, it is like homogenized milk. When the raw milk comes from the farm, a dairy runs it through a homogenizer. As the milk runs through the machine, pistons compact the milk so that the cream and skim milk are made one. As a result you cannot take cream off the milk. In the same way, the human and divine natures of Jesus are compacted into one integrated person.

This means that the Father and the Son are one. When Jesus prays, God also prays. When the human Jesus suffers and dies on a cross, God is in Jesus enduring the cross. "God was in Christ reconciling the world to himself" (2 Corinthians 5:19). When the human Jesus speaks, it is also God who speaks. When Jesus weeps, God weeps. This truth makes us realize the seriousness of the cross. It was not only a human on the cross, but God was there in Jesus. Good Friday is the day God died in Jesus. Indeed, the murderers did not know what they were doing; they did not know they were killing God! As the spiritual says, "Sometimes it causes me to tremble, tremble, tremble."

The Creed's Witness
Not only does the Chalcedon confession witness to the humanity of Jesus, but 350 years earlier the Apostles' Creed did also.

The Name: "I believe in Jesus ..."

When the archangel Gabriel came to Mary to announce that she was chosen by God to be the mother of God's Son, he instructed her to name the baby "Jesus." The Hebrew form of the name is "Joshua." It means, "He shall save."

The name expresses the humanness of Jesus. In Hebrew thought, a name is exceedingly important because it denotes the nature of a person. Therefore, the name of God is not to be used in vain, according to one of the Ten Commandments. The misuse or abuse of the name directly affects the person. A name tells who you are. The name, Jesus, indicates that Jesus was human, born like every human, and grew into manhood. Because of the relation of the name to the person, we pray in the name of Jesus and we hail the power of Jesus' name.

The name, Jesus, is used repeatedly in the monogram IHS, which can be seen on a cross, in stained-glass windows, on paraments, and carved on chancel furnishings. In spite of its wide use, many have no idea what it stands for. For some it means "In His Service," or *In Hoc Signo*, "in this sign." Others think it stands for "1 Hour Service." In a certain church a husband gave altar paraments in memory of his dead wife, Ida Helen Stouffer. After the dedication service, a member asked the pastor whether he did not think that the donor should not have put his wife's initials on the paraments: IHS. These three letters are the first three in the Greek word for Jesus: IHSOUS.

The Birth: "Born of the Virgin Mary"

Mary was the earthly mother of Jesus. She was the mother of no ordinary person. She was the mother of Jesus, the Son of God. In this sense we can say she is the "mother of God." As such we admire, respect, and honor her as the greatest mother that ever lived. Because she was human, Protestants do not pray to her or worship her. Also, Protestants do not accept the Roman Catholic teachings of the Immaculate Conception and the Blessed Assumption. In 1997 *Time* magazine reported the prediction that Pope John Paul II would in 1998 exercise his power of infallibility to declare Mary the Co-Redemptrix of humanity, making her a participant in salvation along with her son Jesus Christ. To Protestants this would mean that Christ was demeaned as the unique Savior.

Not only does the creed say that Mary was the mother of Jesus but that she was the Virgin Mary, referring to the virgin birth. Not all who say this in the creed believe it to be a historical fact. Many have difficulty accepting the virgin birth. The birth involves the doctrine of the Incarnation: God came to earth in the human Jesus. How did he come? The creed explains that Jesus was born of the Virgin Mary. "The Word became flesh" through Mary.

What the Virgin Birth does *not* mean: First, belief in the Virgin Birth is *not* necessary for salvation. One can be a true Christian and not believe in it. Why? Because our salvation does not depend on *how* Jesus was born, but on how he died. The chief symbol of our faith is not a cradle but a cross. The method of Jesus' coming to earth is really peripheral and nonessential for salvation. Our faith is based on his death and resurrection.

Second, the Virgin Birth does not mean that it made Jesus sinless. Some claim that because Jesus was born without a human father, he was free from original sin and consequently he was sinless. Sin is not a physical matter and is not passed down by physical birth. Sin is a spiritual matter involving the mind, heart, and will. Even if Jesus were born free from Joseph's sinful nature, Mary was a sinner and through her Jesus could have inherited original sin. To overcome this, Roman Catholics pronounced the doctrine of the Immaculate Conception, which holds that Mary was born free from original sin.

Third, we need to realize that the Virgin Birth does not imply that parenthood is inherently sinful. It is incorrect to think that sexual intercourse between married mates is dirty and ugly. Sex is God's creation for the continuation of the human race. In the creation of the universe, the Bible tells us that everything God created was good. Therefore, if Joseph and Mary had a loving sexual experience, the child would be pure and honorable.

On the other hand, many do accept the Virgin Birth as truth. Why do they? First, because scripture teaches it. We must admit, however, that Paul, Peter, John, and James do not mention it. Only Matthew and Luke tell the story of the Virgin Birth. Apparently, the Virgin Birth was not important enough to the New Testament writers to refer to it. Moreover, there is no prophecy that forecasts a virgin birth. Matthew 1:23 refers to Isaiah 7:14 as a prophecy of the Virgin Birth. In the Isaiah passage the Hebrew word *Almah* is used, meaning "a woman of marriageable age." When the Septuagint translated the Hebrew into Greek, the word *parthenos,* meaning "virgin," was used. When Matthew quotes Isaiah 7:14, he uses the Greek and not the original Hebrew word. Isaiah 7:14 should be understood in the light of its context. Syria and Israel are about to attack Judah with Ahaz as king. Isaiah urges Ahaz not to go to Egypt for help but to trust God to deliver him from his enemies. Isaiah asks Ahaz to seek a sign that God will do it. Ahaz refuses to ask for a sign. Then Isaiah says that God will do it anyway: a woman will conceive and bear a son whose name is to be Immanuel (God with us), and by the time the child knows right from wrong, Ahaz' enemies will be gone. In light of this knowledge, we can see that there is no prophecy of a virgin birth.

Moreover, we can believe in the Virgin Birth because it is a part of the tradition of the Christian church. Already at the time of the Apostles' Creed (100 A.D.) the church was confessing her belief in the Virgin Birth. By the second century the doctrine was universally accepted. For twenty centuries millions upon millions of Christians have held to the doctrine.

In the third place, we can believe in the Virgin Birth because we believe in miracles. The Virgin Birth was a miracle — the wondrous fact that the infinite God came to us as a little baby. This is a little miracle compared to the miracle of the Resurrection, the greatest of all miracles.

Probably the best reason for accepting the Virgin Birth is its theological significance. It tells us that Jesus is the product of God and not man. God took the initiative through grace to come to the world in Jesus as his last desperate effort to reconcile the world to himself. How does one explain a perfect, sinless life like Jesus? The Virgin Birth explains that Jesus is of God and from God. He is absolutely unique among all human beings, past, present, and future. There is none like him. There was no birth like his. The Virgin Birth is a special birth for a super-special person.

The Significance Of Jesus' Humanity

What did it mean for Jesus to be human? The creed has Jesus born of a virgin. Now he is fully human. What did it mean to him to be born of a virgin and share our humanity? In Philippians 2 Paul tells us that in his leaving heaven for earth, Jesus "emptied himself, taking the form of a servant ... humbled himself, and became obedient unto death, even the death of a cross." In becoming human Jesus was subject to the trials and tribulations, the hunger and thirst, the violence at the hands of wicked people.

It meant suffering for Jesus as the creed says "suffered under Pontius Pilate." This does not mean his suffering was limited to persecution at the hands of Pilate. His is the only name other than Jesus in the Apostles' Creed. Christians never want to forget this Roman governor who, out of cowardice and political expediency, had Jesus tortured and sentenced to death at the insistence of the Jewish mob. His name in the creed is perhaps Pilate's punishment, for millions upon millions each Sunday for 2,000 years have spoken his name and his crime. Because he was human, Jesus suffered like all humans do: the injustice of the courts, the pain of bigotry, and the tragedy of religious fanaticism.

Jesus' being human meant crucifixion as the creed says "was crucified." The creed tells us how he died. He did not die of old age, or of sickness, or by accident. He was murdered. He died the most horrible death — a slow, torturous death on a cross reserved by the Romans for traitors and criminals. He suffered the worst that humankind could do to another human. It meant death and burial as the creed says "dead and buried." Jesus really and truly died. He was as dead as dead can be. As a human, he shared fully with all human beings the last enemy, death. And, of course, he was buried in a tomb borrowed from Joseph of Arimathea. Here ends the human Jesus!

The Human Jesus

When Jimmy Carter was running for President of the United States, he was not known by many people. Often when his name was mentioned, the reaction was "Jimmy who?" For ages, even today, people have been asking, "Jesus who?" Jesus presented the same question to his disciples at Caesarea Philippi, "Who do you say I am?" Do you agree with Peter's answer? Read Matthew 16:13-20.

What do you think of Jesus? Check your answers and double-check the most complete answer:

1. ___ Jesus is only a human.
2. ___ Jesus is a reflection of God.
3. ___ Jesus is the Word of God incarnate.
4. ___ Jesus is a prophet endowed with the spirit of God.
5. ___ Jesus is a divine soul in a human body.
6. ___ Jesus is true God in the form of a true man.
7. ___ Jesus is the personification of perfect humanity.

The Human Jesus In The Creed

Find the human Jesus in the second article of the creed. Quote the creed's answers:

1. _____
2. _____
3. _____
4. _____
5. _____
6. _____

The Name Of Jesus
1. Who gave Jesus his name? Read Luke 1:29-31.
2. What does Jesus' name mean? Read Matthew 1:21.
3. In whose name do we pray? Read John 14:14.
4. By what name are we saved? Read Acts 4:12.

The Virgin Birth
Like every human Jesus was born of a woman. Unlike every other human, Jesus was born of a virgin. In the following questions, if your answer is YES, check the appropriate question. If you do not know the answer, consult your leader or present the question for discussion.

1, ___ Is belief in the Virgin Birth necessary for salvation?

2. ___ Does the Virgin Birth prove that Jesus was sinless?

3. ___ Does the Virgin Birth indicate that Jesus' birth was totally God's work?

4. ___ Does the Virgin Birth insinuate that normal birth procedures are unclean?

5. ___ Does the Virgin Birth mean that Jesus is unique and different from all other persons because he came directly from God through a godly woman?

Chapter 8

The Divine Christ

Though it is important, it is not enough to say that Jesus was a fully human being. The New Testament witnesses to the truth that Jesus Christ is the only Son of God. Mark, the earliest Gospel, begins, "In the beginning of the good news of Jesus Christ, the Son of God." John ends his Gospel: "But these are written so that you may come to believe that Jesus is the Messiah, the Son of God." According to the Bible and the creed Jesus is the theanthropic person, that is, the God-man. In the last chapter we considered the human Jesus; now we turn to study the divine Christ.

1. **The Divine Name:** Christ
The creed says, "I believe in Jesus Christ." Some erroneously think that "Jesus" was his first name and "Christ" is his family name, similar to "John Doe." As "Jesus" stood for his human nature, "Christ" refers to his divine nature.

The word "Christ" is a title given by the church meaning "the anointed one." He is God's Messiah (Hebrew) or Redeemer (Greek). He is God's servant called and sent to redeem the world. It is proper then to say "Jesus the Christ" — Messiah, Redeemer, Savior, God's Son.

His name, "Christ," is often seen in the symbolism of our churches. As IHS stood for "Jesus," so the monogram *Chi Rho* for Christ. *Chi Rho* (XP or P over X) consists of the first two Greek letters of the word, "Christ" (*Xpistos*). Similar to IHS, *Chi Rho* can be seen on crosses, in stained-glass, on paraments and chancel furnishings.

2. **The Divine Relationship:** "His only Son"
The most distinctive and unique characteristic of Jesus was his relationship with God. At both his baptism and transfiguration, God calls him his son: "You are my beloved son." "Son" indicates a

family association. In a family we are one: same blood, same concerns, same love and caring. Husband and wife are one flesh and children are of the same flesh. Jesus said, "The Father and I are one" (John 10:30). Because he shares the same nature as God, he is truly God as well as man.

Is Jesus "a" or "the" Son? In the movie *Oh, God*, George Burns, playing the part of God, is asked whether he has a son. He replies, "I have a number of sons: Moses, Jesus, Mohammed, Buddha ..." This answer is not in accord with the Bible nor the creed. Jesus Christ is "his only Son"; the key word is "only." Paul wrote, "There is one Lord, one faith, one baptism, one God" (Ephesians 4:5-6). Christ is the one and only way to God the Father (John 14:6).

How then should we Christians consider the non-Christian religions? We acknowledge that there are moral values and spiritual insights in non-Christian religions. God has given his witness in various ways, times, and peoples. But his perfect and final witness is in his only Son, Jesus Christ. Other religions are like various rays of the sun, but God's only Son is the sun itself. Other religions seek God but in Christianity God seeks humankind. This seeking occurs when the church goes into all the world with the gospel.

3. **The Divine Origin:** "Conceived by the Holy Spirit"; "Conceived by the Power of the Holy Spirit"

According to this phrase in the creed, Jesus was God and had God in him from the beginning of his earthly existence. He did not come as a human reproductive accident. He was no unwanted child. God was the source of his being. The Spirit, the third person of the Trinity, created him in the womb of Mary. Unlike us, Jesus was not a religiously adopted child. He was God's child from the very beginning. Before he was born, he existed with the Father in heaven. The Spirit caused the eternal Christ to take human form, so that he could live as a physical being on earth and could identify with humanity.

4. **The Divine Descent:** "He descended into hell"; "He descended to the dead"

Jesus died on a cross and was buried in the new tomb of Joseph of Arimathea. When his body was in the tomb, where was Jesus? Did you ever wonder about that? He was not in heaven, for

Luke tells us he ascended forty days after the resurrection. Was he in hell? But why would a sinless person go there? Did he go to the dead? Are the dead in hell? Again, did you ever wonder about the people who lived before Christ? If we believe that we are saved by grace through faith in Christ, how could those living before Jesus ever have the chance to accept him as Savior? This doctrine of the descensus will help us get the answers. Although the church has always believed in this doctrine, it was not enunciated until 359 A.D. in the Symbol of Sirmiurn and officially became part of the Apostles' Creed in 570 A.D.

According to the scriptures, Jesus did NOT go to hell. The traditional version of the creed follows the King James Version which uses the word "hell." "Hell" is used for two Hebrew words, *Gehenna* and *Sheol*. *Gehenna* is the Hebrew word for "hell." It refers to he Valley of Hinnom located outside Jerusalem. It was the garbage dump and incinerator that constantly burned. It stood for a place of misery, torture, and punishment. Sheol is the place of the dead located under the earth. The Bible refers to a three-story universe as follows: the heavens, the earth under the heavens, and Sheol under the earth. In Philippians 2:10 Paul refers to this kind of universe: "At the name of Jesus every knee should bend, in heaven and on earth and under the earth." Sheol was a shadowy place, devoid of light, joy, and peace. It was often referred to as the "pit." Job described it: "Before I go whence I shall not return, to the land of gloom and deep darkness, the land of gloom and chaos, where light is as darkness" (Job 10:21-22). The worst part about Sheol was that there was no escape, no life after death. The first reference to life after death came in the second century before Christ in Daniel 12:2. Even at the time of Jesus, not all believed in life after death. A major religious party, the Sadducees, did not believe. They tried to trick Jesus by asking him about a woman who had seven husbands and which one would be her husband after death.

The contemporary version of the creed is correct by saying, "He descended to the dead." His going to the dead in Sheol is referred to in Acts 2:27; Romans 10:6-7; Ephesians 4:8-10; Revelation 5:13; John 5:25; and especially 1 Peter 3:19 and 4:6. Why did

;us go to the dead? According to 1 Peter 3:19 and 4:6, he went to tell the dead of his victory over Satan, sin, and death. The price of humanity's redemption was paid. The work of salvation was completed. He gave them the good news that they, too, could accept him and go with him to heaven. The dead includes all people, Jews and Gentiles, who lived before him. In the painting by Fra Angelico of the fifteenth century (see page 109), we see the resurrected Jesus carrying the banner of victory. The stone slab was broken down and fell on Satan. The dead, including all people (notice the haloes), come to Christ for deliverance.

What happens when we die? Where do we go? Perhaps the following diagram will help us to understand.

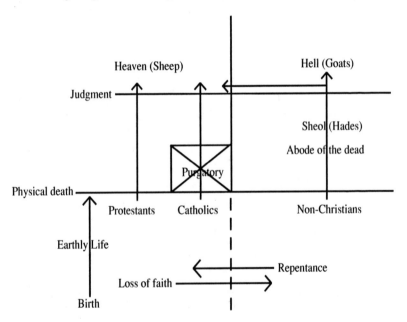

Explanation Of The Diagram

We begin with life on earth by birth. Life on earth may last as long as 100 or more years, ending with physical death. On earth

Fra Angelico 1387-1455

are Christians and non-Christians; both die. Before death it is possible for the non-Christian to cross over and become a Christian; a Christian can lose faith and go over to the non-Christian side. Note the broken line indicating the possibility of crossing over. After death there is no crossover. Note the solid line after death. After death the Bible says there is no repentance, no crossover. It is here and now that we choose where to spend eternity, either heaven or hell.

When people die, where are they? What is the next thing to happen? The New Testament tells us that Christ will return at an unknown date to judge the living and the dead. Then he will decide who goes to heaven or hell. Until that time non-Christians remain in Sheol for the judgment. At death Christians go to be with Jesus and have eternal life in heaven. For Protestants this is direct and immediate. According to Roman Catholic teaching, Catholics go to Purgatory to be prepared for heaven. Purgatory is a teaching of the Roman Church and is not in the Bible. Consequently, Protestants do not accept it. Purgatory was introduced by Pope Gregory the Great in the sixth century and became a dogma at the Council of Trent in 1563 A.D. According to Rome, a person needs Purgatory to prepare for heaven. Restitution must be made for sins confessed. A priest at private confession prescribes the punishment known as penance. Time in Purgatory may be shortened by indulgences, which were a remission of temporal punishment. Purgatory is viewed as a fire that burns away sins. At a Roman Catholic funeral service the following prayer was offered: "Be not severe in Thy judgment but let some drops of Thy precious blood fall upon the devouring flames."

5. **The Divine Miracle:** "The third day he rose again from the dead"; "On the third day he rose again"

The resurrection was a divine miracle, for God raised up Jesus from the dead. This "third day" was the great day of history. It is further evidence for the deity of Jesus. If he were only human, he would have died like every other human. Consider the importance of this day we call Easter. The resurrection changed the Sabbath to the Lord's Day, and ever since that day, millions upon millions of Christians meet on the first day of the week to celebrate the event.

Now people have assurance of victory: life over death, hope over despair, truth over falsehood, and love over hatred.

The importance of the resurrection can be seen if we ask, what if Christ had not risen? In 1 Corinthians 15, Paul says that if Christ had not risen, our preaching would be in vain; our faith likewise would be in vain. We would still be in our sins, the dead would have perished, and our hardships endured for Christ would be in vain.

Without the resurrection the Christian religion would collapse. It is the keystone in the arch of the Christian faith. If Christ had not risen, he would be only a martyr to a good cause and not the Savior. His promises of forgiveness and eternal life would have no effect. His teachings would still be good but without authority. Without the resurrection Christianity would be just another religion with helpful teachings and ethical principles. The cross would be without power to save, a tragedy and not a victory. Because of Easter, Christianity as a religion is unique. The leaders of all other religions died and remain dead. Only Jesus rose from the dead and lives now and for eternity. Does that tell us which religion is the true one?

In light of the supreme importance of the resurrection, we need to ask, "Did Jesus really rise from the dead or do we only believe he did? Did he rise physically or did he just rise in the minds of the disciples?" Many Americans think Elvis Presley is alive even though his body is buried in the garden of his mansion. Is Jesus really alive or do we just think he lives? Saint Paul wrote, "In fact Christ has been raised from the dead" (1 Corinthians 15:20). The resurrection is a fact and not fiction. The nature of his resurrected body is secondary. According to the Gospels, it was a mysterious, glorified body that was both physical and spiritual.

But, you ask, how can we be sure he rose? There is the empty tomb but it is no absolute guarantee of the resurrection. A more certain proof is the experience that people from the beginning and through history had with the risen Jesus. Then there is the testimony of the church through the ages. Without the risen Christ, the church would disappear. The final proof is one's own personal experience: "I know he lives, because he lives in my heart."

6. **The Divine Ascension:** "He ascended into heaven"

The scene is glorious! Having completed his work and humili-ation with suffering, God's Son is welcomed home by his Father and the angels. We can see the Son coming with bands playing, angelic choirs singing, trumpets blaring, and banners waving! What a glorious reception with God the Father standing before his throne with outstretched arms welcoming his faithful and obedient Son! Jesus Christ now returns to his former glory, honor, and power which he had before the Incarnation.

The Ascension has been portrayed in the creed, in painting, and on stained-glass windows. From the first century the Ascen-sion has been in scripture and in the worship of the church. In my own case, the Ascension made a deep impression on my life. In the church where I grew up, there was a painting of the ascending Christ on the reredos above the altar. Later when I went to semi-nary, I saw each day the Ascension in the stained-glass window above the altar with Jesus giving the final mandate to go into all the world and preach the gospel.

The Ascension is a problem for those who take it literally. It implies an anthropomorphic conception of God. Indeed, God does not have a literal right hand where Jesus is seated. Moreover, the Ascension is placed in a three-story universe. In our space age we know there is no up and no down. The ascending Jesus did not have a physical body. The Ascension is simply telling us that Christ returned to his Father and resumed his role as Son of God, King of kings, and ruler of the universe. Christ was exalted and all things were put under his feet.

What does the Ascension mean to us today? It means, for one thing, Jesus can be with us wherever we are. When he was on earth, he was limited by time and space. His ministry was limited to one race and one country. Now he is available at any time and any place for anyone who calls upon him. Now it is possible for Jesus' promise to come true: "I am with you always."

It also means that Jesus sits at the right hand of God as our high priest. He is next to God the Father and intercedes for us. We come to God through Jesus. When we pray, we offer our petitions in his name. When we appear before God for forgiveness, Jesus is our Advocate.

In addition, Jesus' going to heaven gives the church a challenge to complete the work of saving the world by making disciples of the nations. He has given his followers the ministry of reconciliation.

Only because Jesus ascended, the Holy Spirit is received. Christ comes to us and lives in us by the Holy Spirit. Through his Spirit we are guided into truth and empowered to do his will.

7. **The Divine Judgment:** "From thence he shall come to judge the quick and the dead;" "He will come again to judge the living and the dead"

Only God can judge the nations and send people to heaven or hell. "He shall come again to judge...." The "he" in the creed is Jesus. Because he is the Son of God, he will return to earth to judge the world at an unknown time.

His coming to judge means the winding up of history. His coming, the Parousia, teaches us that history has meaning. History has a meaning, an ending with God. It is not a mere running down until it lacks momentum. Nor is it an endless repeating of cycles, cycles of history repeating itself. This is God's world and Christians believe God has a purpose for the world. He will end it when it is his will to do so.

Moreover, Christ's return means there will be a settling of accounts. On earth the good have not always been rewarded and the wicked have not been punished. When he returns, things will be straightened out and all will get their just desserts. Therefore, the people of God will rejoice when he comes. Until he comes, they pray, "Maranatha," "Come, Lord Jesus, come quickly."

Judgment: Now Or Later

Judgment is universal: both the living and the dead. "For all of us must appear before the judgment seat of Christ" (2 Corinthians 5:10). Everyone will be required to give an account of his/her stewardship. We will be asked, "What have you done with your life?"

The big question is WHEN will the judgment occur — now or later when Jesus returns at the end of time? For non-Christians the answer is "later." Paul writes: "By your hard and impenitent heart you are storing up wrath when God's righteous judgment will be revealed" (Romans 2:5). Until Christ returns non-Christians will wait in Sheol (Hades) for final judgment.

The time of judgment for Christians is both: now and later. They who hold to the "later" view believe the dead sleep in their graves. At the sound of the trumpet, Christ will return and the dead will rise for the judgment. "For the trumpet will sound and the dead will be raised imperishable, and we will be changed" (1 Corinthians 15:52). This view presents some questions: (1) If this is true, how then can a pastor say at a funeral of a Christian that the deceased is with Jesus in heaven? (2) In the case of cremation, how would ashes become the original physical body?

Another view is that Christians are judged here and now before they die. We have the witness of Jesus: "Truly, truly I say to you, he who hears my word and believes him who sent me, *has* eternal life" (John 5:24). Again, Jesus said, "Those who believe in him are *not* condemned" (John 3:18). Jesus said to the repentant thief on the cross: "Today you will be with me in paradise" (Luke 23:43).

Paul also takes the position that a Christian is judged now. He wrote, "There is therefore now no condemnation for those who are in Christ Jesus" (Romans 8:1). In Philippians 1:21, 23 Paul confesses, "For me to live is Christ and to die is gain. My desire is to be with Christ, for that is far better."

If, from these passages, we learn that at death Christians go directly and immediately to be with Christ in heaven, why would there be a future judgment for them? To be with Christ, we would have to be forgiven and accepted. Judgment comes to Christians here and now. It occurs when we confess our sins and receive absolution of our sins, especially when we receive the sacraments.

Saint Paul gives us a second reason for believing judgment of Christians takes place now, not later. If at death Christians go to be with their Lord in heaven, they are with him when he decides to return to earth to judge. In 1 Thessalonians Paul says, "God will bring with him those who have died" (4:14). Then when Christ and his people come to earth for the judgment of the nations, Christians on earth at the time "will be caught up in the clouds together with them to meet the Lord in the air, and so we will be with the Lord forever" (4:17). Some call this meeting the "rapture."

A third reason for holding to the view that Christians face judgment now, not later, is in the wonderful fact that God forgets when he forgives. Isaiah teaches us this truth: "I am he who blots out your transgressions for my own sake, and I will *not remember* your sins" (43:25). When we confess our sins and receive forgiveness, the sin is forever blotted out and will never again be brought against us. A story is told of a priest who had an exceptional nun who claimed she often talked with God. One day the priest asked her to ask God what was the secret sin of their bishop. She agreed to ask God. Some time later the priest asked the nun if she talked with God and gave him the question. She replied that she did. He said, "What did God say that the bishop's secret sin was?" She answered, "God said he forgot." It must be like an audio or video tape. When it is reused, the original is automatically erased. Isn't this good news? At the thought of dying, I dreaded the possibility of having to appear before God and confess every word said and every deed done. It has taken away the fear of judgment.

What does this present judgment mean to us? Does it not mean that the last thing we should do before dying is to confess our sins and receive God's forgiveness? The church offers this service by administering to the dying the sacrament of the Holy Communion when we receive the remission of our sins.

It means also that we need to live daily in a state of grace. Be right with God every day so that we can say, "It is well with my soul." Then it does not matter when we die. We can face death without terror or fear. It is a wonderful feeling to know that we are right with the Judge and we have the assurance of heaven. We can look forward to death as a meeting with Jesus and for a reunion with the loved ones who preceded us in death.

Study Guide

The Divine Christ

The Divine Name
1. Who gave Jesus his name? Check your answer(s).
   ___ Father
   ___ Mother
   ___ Gabriel (See Luke 1:26, 31)
   ___ God

2. If Jesus is his name, where did "Christ" originate? Check your answer.
   ___ Peter (See Matthew 16:16)
   ___ Jesus' enemies: Pharisees, Sadducees (See Matthew 27:22)
   ___ Church: a title but not a name (See 1 John 2:22)

Descent To Hell
   The traditional version of the Apostles' Creed says that Jesus "descended into hell." Can you accept that? Check your answers.
1. ___ Because Jesus was sinless, Jesus never went to hell.
2. ___ Jesus went to hell to suffer hell for us.
3. ___ I believe Jesus went to hell because the Bible says so.
4. ___ Jesus did not go to hell but to Sheol, to the dead.
5. ___ Jesus went to Sheol to proclaim his victory over death and Satan.
6. ___ By going to Sheol, Jesus opened the gate of heaven to all who died.

Because He Was God
   Only one who was God could do the following. Look up the passages and write the answers.
1. Be conceived by the _____ _____. (Luke 1:35)
2. Rise from the _____. (Mark 16:6)

3. _____ to heaven. (Luke 24:51)
4. Sit at the _____ hand of God. (Acts 2:33)
5. Promise to return to _____ all people. (Matthew 25:31-33)

A Study Of Sheol

Is Sheol a strange word for you? Have you ever heard of it? Read the following passages and give a description in the blanks:
1. Job 10:21-22 _____
2. Acts 2:27 _____
3. Romans 10:6-7 _____
4. Ephesians 4:8-10 _____
5. 1 Peter 3:19, 4:6 _____
6. Jude 6 _____

A Painting Of Sheol By Fra Angelico

Please turn to the picture on page 109 and study it. Can you find the answers to the following questions?
1. Who is the person welcoming the dead?

2. What does the flag signify?

3. Where is Satan?

4. Who are those wearing haloes?

5. On what is the resurrected Christ standing?

6. Where are the dead?

Chapter 9

Christ The Redeemer

Some years ago a Japanese business executive living in South America was kidnapped. His captors demanded a ransom of a million dollars. If it was not paid, the executive would be killed. The ransom was paid and the man was freed and restored to his family. In a similar way humanity is a captive of Satan and threatened with death. Christ gives his life on the cross as a ransom that sinners might be redeemed from sin, death, and hell. As God the Father's work was the creation of the universe, God the Son's work was the redemption of humanity. The Apostles' Creed sums it up: "He suffered under Pontius Pilate, was crucified, died, and was buried."

Christ came to redeem us, to save us. Paul wrote: "Christ Jesus came into the world to save sinners" (1 Timothy 1:15). What does it mean to be saved? What does redemption mean to you? The following diagram may help us understand Christ's work of redemption. It calls for an understanding of the condition of humanity before and after humankind's fall from God and Christ's work of redemption to restore us to our original status.

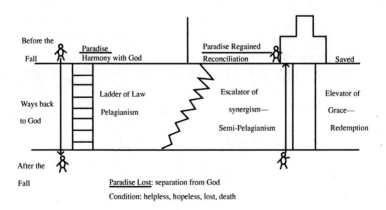

119

Paradise

When God created Adam and Eve, they were in a perfect relationship with their Creator. The Garden of Eden was a paradise. God and his creation were in perfect harmony and peace. God and his original people were one. Communication between them was ideal. There was no sin to disturb the divine-human relationship. Our first parents were what we would call today "saved." They were right with God. This is the way God intended it to be for all time. In this relationship, the human pair enjoyed life, peace, and joy. For a description of this condition, please read the first two chapters of Genesis.

Paradise Lost

Then something dreadful happened. Humanity fell from this perfect relationship with God. Sin entered the relationship and all was lost. Satan tempted Eve to disobey God by eating the forbidden fruit. After she yielded to the temptation, she persuaded Adam to do the same. The result? At once they became afraid of God. They had a sense of guilt and lost their innocence, symbolized by their making clothes for themselves out of fig leaves. The consequence of their sin was expulsion from the garden and separation from God. They lost their paradise (Genesis 3).

As a result of disobedience, humanity represented in Adam and Eve was separated from God. Sin always separates God from a person and separates people from people. Daily experience testifies to this. When someone sins against us, hurts us, talks about us, plays a dirty trick on us, or does us an injustice, we become estranged. We have a falling out, just as humanity had a falling down from paradise. We are no longer on speaking terms. We are angry and may seek revenge. We are no longer friends but enemies. This condition exists until one or both parties apologize and ask for forgiveness.

It is the same in our relationship with God. Sin broke it. We have fallen away from God. A great chasm divides us. What is our condition in this fallen state? We are helpless to stop sinning. We are hopeless in that we can never make things right with God. Sin always brings suffering, and the wages of sin is death. We as sinners are in a state of total despair. This is what is meant by "lost." We are in the grip of sin, Satan, and death. We are the slaves of sin.

Is this the case in today's world? Do we sin? Our society is saturated with sin. It is so common that we take sin for granted. It is the normal way of life. For proof take a look at your daily newspaper, a tabloid of sin, crime, drugs, murder, theft, sexual abuse, and infidelity. Yet not all people admit they are sinners. In a poll of 1,472 church members, 57 percent said all are sinners; 43 percent deny it. In contrast, Saint Paul held that all are born under the power of sin (Romans 3:9). The Psalmist declares, "In sin did my mother conceive me" (Psalm 51:5). In his first letter John says, "If we say we have no sin, we deceive ourselves and the truth is not in us" (1:8). As a result all humanity is diseased with sin. All of us are sinful because humanity is one body. Sin entered the body through Adam and Eve. We are by nature sinful and unclean. We are by nature rebels against God and we cannot help but sin.

Sin is of two kinds: original and actual. We commit actual sins by thought, word, and deed. Most of us readily admit this and our daily newscasts confirm it. There is a difference between sins and SIN. Sin is original sin, the cause of our sins. Original sin goes back to our first parents and their sin of disobedience. It is like a bucket of water in which a drop of blueing scatters and the whole bucket is contaminated. Ralph Waldo Emerson agreed, "Everything in nature is cracked." George Bernard Shaw recognized original sin as the only empirically verifiable Christian doctrine. After 25 years as a jeweler, a man decided to retire and move to Florida. A tourist noticed he had a beautiful diamond ring and remarked, "That is a perfectly beautiful diamond ring." The former jeweler explained, "It is the only thing I kept from the jewelry business. It is beautiful, but it is not perfect. Only human-made, industrial diamonds are perfect. The ones God made, like this one, all have a flaw in them." Each of us is born with a flaw which we call original sin.

This brings up the question whether children are born good or bad. Some people look at a baby and say it is good. Indeed, a newborn baby has not committed actual sin in terms of thought, word, or deed. But a child has original sin in terms of a disposition to sin.

Sinful parents produce sinful children. Parents can see it in their children. Do parents ever have to say to their children, "Be bad"? The first word of a child is "NO." The first sentence is "That's not fair." Later comes, "Don't blame me. I didn't do it." When I was a seminary student, some of us did not accept the doctrine of original sin. Our professor of theology said, "I know some of you do not believe in original sin. Just wait until you are parents and you will believe it!" Because children are born in sin, it is necessary for them to be disciplined. Because babies need to become by adoption children of God and forgiven of original sin, the church for ages has practiced infant baptism.

Sin expresses itself in two ways: omission and commission. Many of us think of sin in terms of commission: what we say and what we do is wrong. Often we fail to see our sins of omission. It is not what we say or do but what we do not say or do when we have the opportunity. There is a tendency to blame Eve for the original sin. But Adam was equally guilty. She committed the sin of commission and Adam committed the sin of omission. Why did he not convince Eve that it was wrong to disobey God? Why did he not exercise his headship by forbidding her to eat the fruit? In the biblical record, there is absolute silence from Adam. By his silence, he agreed with Eve. Consider also the disciples' sin of omission. When Jesus was arrested and on trial for his life, the disciples forsook him and fled. Why did they not defend him and witness in his behalf? In the light of this, we need to cry out with Luther, "My sins! My sins!" *Mea culpa!*

What To Do About Sin

In the light of the fact that we all are sinners, what can we do about it? The answer is in one word given by Jesus: "Repent." The word comes from the Greek *metanoia*, meaning a change of mind, a change of allegiance from Satan to God, a change of life from wickedness to godliness, a change of heart from hatred to love.

This repentance is expressed in the confession of sins. We will confess to others whom we offended and mistreated. We will say, "I am sorry. I apologize. It was my fault." The Prodigal Son repented by returning home to his father. The first thing the son said was "Father, I have sinned against heaven and before you" (Luke 15:21). Sins against people are at the same time sins against God. David sinned against Bathsheba and her husband Uriah, but when the prophet Nathan confronted him with the crime, David confessed to God: "I have sinned against the Lord" (2 Samuel 12:13). The liturgy of the church provides us with a prayer of confession to God:

> *O God, our heavenly Father, I confess to you that I have grievously sinned against you in many ways; not only by outward transgressions but also by secret thoughts and desires which I cannot fully understand, but which are all known to you. I do earnestly repent, and am heartily sorry for these my offenses and I beseech you of your great goodness to have mercy upon me, and for the sake of your dear Son, Jesus Christ our Lord, to forgive my sins, and graciously to help my infirmities.*

After confession of sins, we petition God for forgiveness. Our prayer is "Lord, have mercy; Christ, have mercy; Lord, have mercy." His mercy is offered when the ordained minister says:

> *Almighty God, in his mercy, has given his Son to die for us and, for his sake, forgives us all our sins. As a called and ordained minister of the Church of Christ, and by his authority, I therefore declare to you the entire forgiveness of all your sins, in the name of the Father, and of the Son, and of the Holy Spirit.*

Having received pardon, we now make restitution when possible. The repentant thief on the cross could not make restitution, for he was dying. When Zacchaeus committed himself to Christ, he said, "Look, half of my possessions, Lord, I will give to the poor, and if I have defrauded anyone of anything, I will pay back four times as much" (Luke 19:8).

123

Paradise Regained

Sin caused us to lose paradise. By faith we can regain it through the redemptive work of Christ on the cross. The word "redemption" occurs 152 times in the Bible. It means to buy back, as a slave can be bought for freedom. In like manner, Paul claims Christ bought us out of the slavery of sin, for he wrote: "You were bought with a price" (1 Corinthians 6:20).

What is the most important and essential question a human can ask? In the light of the diagram on page 119, it is: "How can we get back with God? How can we get right with God? Who will deliver us from this body of sin, from the power of Satan, and from the threat of hell?" It is the question of the Philippian jailor who asked Paul and Silas, "Sirs, what must I do to be saved?" (Acts 16:30). The rich young ruler brought the question to Jesus, "Teacher, what good deed must I do to have eternal life?" (Matthew 19:16). How to get right with God has been humankind's search from the beginning of history. Fallen humanity has tried one of at least three ways. Please consult the diagram on page 119.

1. The Ladder

People are trying to get back to God and getting accepted by their works of righteousness. This attempt may be considered as a ladder stretching from earth to heaven. Each rung on the ladder is a law of God. A person reasons: if I obey the laws of God, he will be pleased and I will be accepted as an obedient child. So I start with the first rung, and when I obey it perfectly, I go to the next higher rung. Each higher rung brings me closer to God. If I keep it up and obey perfectly all of the laws, I will be on the top of the ladder and back with God.

No doubt this is a possible way to get right with God, but it is most improbable. To succeed in this method would mean that I would be morally perfect. But who, except Jesus, was ever or will ever be perfect? A pastor once asked a group, "Did you ever know of a perfect person?" A man in the back raised his hand. The pastor continued, "You say you know of a perfect person? Who was it?" The man answered, "My wife's first husband!"

This way to God is an impossible way, for no one can keep all the laws of God. Therefore, Paul calls this "works righteousness," the curse of the law. He calls it a curse because the law requires you to do what you cannot do. Your very best is not good enough. The Greek mythological character, Sisyphus, was condemned by the gods to roll a huge stone up a mountain. Just when he had it at the top, it rolled down again. For eternity his punishment was to roll the stone to the top, but every time it rolled back. He had to do what he could not do. Likewise, to obey every law of God perfectly is a curse because we cannot do it. The ladder is no way to get back to God.

Yet in a poll of 1,472 church members 71 percent indicated that they were saved by doing good works. This view is often expressed by the remark concerning a deceased person: "I know he is in heaven because he was such a good man." We do not get to heaven because we were good or did good. In God's sight our good works are no more than filthy rags. Where then does the law fit into the Christian's life? Are Christians antinomian, that is, against the law? Are we a lawless people? If we are saved by grace, what is the purpose of the law? It has a threefold purpose. First, the law is used as a standard. It shows us that we are sinners in need of redemption. Paul asks, "Why then the law? It was added because of transgressions ..." (Galatians 3:19). We compare our lives with the commandments and realize we disobey all ten of them. The law thus drives us to Christ for forgiveness.

Second, the law is used as a guide for how to live righteously. The law tells us what God requires of us. The law is positive in telling us what God wants us to do and how we are to live with God's approval. For instance, the first commandment of the decalogue tells us, "Put God first in your life."

Third, the law serves as a deterrent against wrongdoing. We need laws to discourage crime. Disobedience to civil laws brings punishment. Keeping the laws promotes a safe and civilized society. It is like a traffic light at a busy intersection. Without the light, there would be accidents with the loss of life.

But we do not obey God's laws to be saved; we obey them because we are already saved. We keep the laws of God out of gratitude for all God has done for us in Christ by redeeming us. We do good works not to win God's favor but to serve the world in his name. The grace of God prompts us to serve and live righteously.

2. **The Escalator**

A second way people try to get right with God is by using an escalator of synergism or semi-Pelagianism. Pelagianism is the view that you can save yourself by your good deeds; semi-Pelagianism says you can save yourself with God's help. Have you ever seen a person who was in a hurry on an escalator? He/she walked up the escalator while it was in motion. The person was getting up by his/her own effort plus the power of the escalator.

The reason for this method to get back to God is that it is evident one cannot keep all the laws. To get to the top we need God's help. We will be saved not only by works but by faith. With God's help we can make it, so we say. This view is based on the false idea that humanity is basically good and needs only a little assistance. The great pianist Paderewski was once scheduled to give a concert. Before he came to the stage, a young boy slipped away from his parents and went to the piano. While the boy was trying to play, Paderewski appeared to begin his concert. He put his arms around the boy and urged him to continue. He said, "Keep on playing and I'll make up the rest."

Do people try to use this way to God? Eighty-two percent of Americans believe "God helps those who help themselves." In a poll of 1,472 church members 76 percent agreed with the statement: "As long as I do the best I can, I feel God cares for me and watches over me." The medieval church taught synergism of faith and works. People were taught that good works were essential to salvation and the church provided the strength to do them through the seven sacraments.

The escalator way of salvation is another impossible way. The fault with this plan is that it is basically the ladder method. In no way can one be pleasing to God, even with a little help from God. Either God must do it all or a person must do it all. Our part would be so minimal that, even with God's help, we could never make ourselves acceptable to God.

3. The Elevator

The other two ways to God we found to be impossible. Now we will try the elevator of grace. It is the good news of the gospel. The good news is that what we could not do for ourselves, God has done for us in Christ. Christ came from heaven to identify totally with sinful humanity by becoming sin for us. He fulfilled the law on our behalf so that we need not obey the law to get right with God. He made the sacrifice by dying for our sins. Now Christ comes to us and says, "Come to me and I will take you to my Father and make all things right with him." He puts on us his precious robe of righteousness to cover up the filthy rags of our sin. Because of Christ's merits and sacrifice, God accepts us, forgives us, and reckons us to be righteous or justified. The goodness of Christ is imputed to us. God declares we are forgiven and that we are his children. This is known as justification by grace through faith, the one indispensable doctrine of the Christian faith. Now we are back with God in peace and joy. We are now "saved" because we have been redeemed, reconciled, and put in right relationship with God. It is not that we are accepted for who we are, what we have, or what we have done. We are saved by grace alone. "For by grace you have been saved through faith, and this is not your own doing; it is the gift of God" (Ephesians 2:8).

All of this is like an elevator. By its own power, it lifts us to a higher story. Christ comes down the elevator of grace through the Incarnation and bids us get on the elevator to go up to God for acceptance. What does it take to get on the elevator? First, you must push the button signaling the desire to use the elevator. It means we must want to be saved, want to go to God to be reconciled. Christ will not force anyone to get on the elevator. It must be your own personal choice. Jesus said, "Come to me." Second, to get on the elevator of grace we must have faith. If you do not have faith that the elevator is safe and will take you up, you will not get on the elevator. Right? It takes faith to get on the elevator of grace, faith that Christ is the Son of God who will make things right with God for you. Third, to get on the elevator, you have to go all the way into the elevator. You cannot have one foot on the elevator and one foot on the floor where you stand. You cannot go halfway with Christ. You go all the way in total commitment and allegiance. We say with the hymn: "Take myself, and I will be/Ever, only, all for Thee."

Now that we have taken the elevator of grace, we are one with God. Having been justified by grace through faith we have peace with God. All is now well with our souls. We are saved, forgiven, redeemed as God's people. This is the wonderful good news of the gospel. Thanks be to God for Christ, our Redeemer!

Pictures Of The Passion

We have just learned of the wonderful good news of Christ the Redeemer who died to free us from sin and death in order that we might be the children of God. How did it happen? What happened on the cross was not a mere subjective experience. Some see in the cross a display of God's love, and this melts our hard hearts to love him in return. According to this view, God is one of justice and wrath, a God who needs to be placated and appeased. In the light of the cross, we change our minds about God. Now we see him as a God of mercy.

The atonement (at-one-ment with God) was a far more radical event than a change in attitude. A very radical change takes place in the relationship between God and humanity. The human race must change from being enemies to friends of God. The cross did not change God's mind to forgive and love humanity. God has always, even before the cross, assured people of God's steadfast love and forgiveness. "The Lord is merciful and gracious, slow to anger and abounding in steadfast love" (Psalm 103:8). It was not God who needed to be reconciled, but humankind which needed to repent and return to God for forgiveness, just as the Prodigal returned to his waiting father.

What caused this change that sinners are forgiven and restored to fellowship with God? There is no one perfect explanation, but various pictures have been suggested as possible explanations.

1. A Courtroom

A cosmic courtroom is the place for human salvation. God the Father is the judge. The human is the convict. Jesus is the advocate for the sinner. The sinner is found guilty and sentenced to death.

The justice of God must be satisfied. God in Christ paid the penalty. Humankind therefore is pronounced acquitted and forgiven. People are now freed from the penalty and power of sin. Therefore, God has declared the believer in Christ righteous or justified.

2. An Altar

In the Old Testament a spotless lamb was sacrificed for the sins of the people. The blood of the lamb removed the stains of sin: "There is power in the blood." The lamb was the substitute for the people who deserved to die. The cross was the altar on which Christ, the spotless Lamb of God, was sacrificed. He was our substitute. As Jesus took the place of Barabbas on the cross, so he takes our place. He died in our behalf. Thus, Jesus was both the victim and the high priest who offered himself as the sacrifice.

3. A Battlefield

From the time of the war in heaven when God cast Satan on earth (Revelation 12:7-12), the battle between God and Satan has continued on earth. God's people are constantly struggling with Satan's temptations and resisting the devil. When Jesus came on earth, Satan saw his chance finally to win the war with God. No one was more sorely tempted than Jesus was. Luther claimed that God used Jesus to catch the devil. The war finally focused on the cross. What seemed like a victory for Satan turned out to be a victory for God, because Jesus finished his work of salvation with a shout of triumph, "It is finished." This victory was confirmed by the glorious resurrection. The victory is celebrated in an Easter hymn:

> *The strife is o'er, the battle's done.*
> *Now is the victor's triumph won!*
> *Now be the song of praise begun.*
> *Alleluia!*

If the battle with Satan was won on the cross, why then does the struggle continue today? The battle was won but the war with Satan continues. In the Civil War the battle of Gettysburg was the battle that won the war, but fighting continued until Appomattox. In like manner, Satan has been defeated. The decisive battle was fought on Calvary. Now we know how the war will end. It is only a matter of time until the end of the conflict. The Christian fights Satan with the assurance of ultimate victory.

Choose the analogy that best suits you, knowing that each analogy is one way of trying to explain the inexplicable. The method does not really matter, does it? We have the most wonderful results of what God did in and through his Son, our blessed Redeemer. Our sins have been covered by the perfect robe of Christ's righteousness. Satisfaction has been made to the God of justice; Christ died in our place and now we live eternally. We have been redeemed from the slavery of sin. God and sinners are reconciled. All this was the work of God the Son, the second person of the Trinity.

The Redeemer And You

What does Jesus Christ mean to you? In our study of the creed thus far, we have learned the nature of Jesus as one who is fully God and fully man. We have been amazed at his work of redemption. So what? What does that mean to you personally? It always comes down to an existential experience, to the very nitty-gritty of life. It is a question none of us can avoid. Jesus did this to his disciples at Caesarea Philippi. It was not so much a matter for the world but for the twelve followers to face and answer. Jesus asked, "Who do you say that I am?" (Matthew 16:15). Consider the following possible answers:

1. **Lord**

What Christ should mean to every Christian is stated in the Apostles' Creed: "I believe in Jesus Christ, his only Son, our *Lord*." It all comes down to one word, "Lord." What does this word mean? In the New Testament, Jesus is called "Lord" 600 times. It is a word packed with meaning. "Lord" implies ownership. He owns us as though we were his property. He owns us because he bought us at the price of his precious blood. He bought us out of slavery to self and sin. "You are not your own; you were bought with a price." Therefore, I am not free to waste, harm, or put an end to my life. I am not free to do with my life as I jolly well please. I am free to belong to Christ and free to serve him, to love and obey him in all things.

2. Master

"Lord," moreover, means "Master." This implies that a Christian is a slave of Christ. We are slaves because he bought us out of slavery of sin to be slaves of righteousness. Paul usually identified himself in his letter as a "servant" of Christ. The Greek word for "servant" is *doulos*, meaning "slave" (Romans 1:1). As a slave a Christian is in his service and obligated to obey his commandments. I will do what he tells me to do, say what he tells me to say, and go where he wants me to go. I have no choice in the matter. And yet I am the freest of all people. In a hymn George Matheson says, "Make me a captive, Lord, and then I shall be free." When we become Christians, we transfer our slavery from Satan to Christ.

3. King

"Lord," in the third place, means "king." Our Lord is the King of kings. A king, as you know, is a sovereign person with full authority and power. If the Lord is our king, we are his subjects. In more common language we could say he is our boss or manager. When we make him Lord of our lives, we voluntarily put our lives under new management. A king has power to enforce his decrees. Jesus said, "All power is given unto me in heaven and earth" (Matthew 28:18). Therefore, our King is able to answer our prayers, to help us out of difficulty, and to overcome our enemies of sin and death. If Jesus is our Lord, he is the most important person in all of history. He is really not our Lord until he comes first in our lives.

4. God

Finally, "Lord" means "God." To say Jesus is our Lord is to say he is our God. "Lord" is used in the Old Testament for "Yahweh." Because of the holiness of God's name, Hebrews refused to say his name for fear of blaspheming it by wrong use. Consequently, they removed the vowels so that the name could not be spoken — YHWH. Scholars added vowels so that we say "Yahweh" or "Jehovah." Since they could not speak God's name, they used as a substitute, *adonai,* meaning "Lord." To call Jesus "Lord," therefore, means that we acknowledge him as the divine Son of God. We can say with Thomas after he was convinced Jesus had risen from the dead, "My Lord and my God!" (John 20:28).

131

Lord To What Extent?

Is Jesus the Lord of our lives, all our lives, or in just a few areas of our lives? In the hymn, "Have Thine Own Way, Lord," we sing, "Hold over my being absolute sway." "Absolute sway" — does Jesus really have complete control and domination of our lives?

We may allow Jesus to be Lord over some areas of our lives, but other areas we hold for ourselves. We may let Jesus be the Lord of our personal lives because we are honest and kind, or Lord of our family life because we are faithful spouses and good parents. Jesus may be Lord of our civic life because we obey the laws and pay our taxes. But what of other areas of our lives? In the area of race, does Christ rule? In the area of finance? Do we tithe our income? In the area of the church, are we faithful in worship, in witnessing for Jesus, in participating in church activities?

To say Jesus is our Lord in the Apostles's Creed means we are in the process of allowing him to be eventually the Lord of all areas of our lives. We are in the process of growth to let Christ have full sway in all areas of life. Each sermon calls for a decision to let Christ enter a new area of life. Each church service is an opportunity to enter into a deeper commitment to Christ.

> *Jesus is all the world to me, my life, my joy, my all,*
> *He is my strength from day to day, without him I would fall.*
> *When I am sad, to him I go, no other one can cheer me so;*
> *When I am sad, he makes me glad, he's my friend.*
> — Will Thompson

A Summary Of The Second Article of The Apostles' Creed

This You Can Believe

I believe that Jesus Christ, true God, begotten of the Father from eternity, and also true man, born of the Virgin Mary, is my Lord; who has redeemed me, a lost and condemned creature, secured and delivered me from all sins, from death and the power of the devil, not with silver and gold, but with his holy and precious blood,

132

and with his innocent sufferings and death, in order that I might be his, live under him in his kingdom, and serve him in everlasting righteousness, innocence, and blessedness, even as he is risen from the dead, and lives and reigns to all eternity. This is most certainly true.
— Martin Luther, *The Small Catechism*

Christ The Redeemer

The Redeemer's Work

In the first article of the Apostles' Creed we learned that the work of God the Father was creation of the universe. What was the work of God the Son? Was there anything left for the Son to do? Why did the Father send his Son to the world? Let Jesus tell us why he came:

1. Read John 10:10 — "I came that they might have _____."
2. Read Luke 19:10 — "The Son of man came to seek and to _____ the lost."
3. Read Matthew 20:28 — "The Son of man came ... to give his life as a _____."

Time To Think

Since the fall of Adam, humanity is in a predicament. The plight of humankind apart from God is pathetic: helpless, hopeless, lost, threatened with suffering, death, and hell. What are your answers to these questions:

1. Is humanity by nature sinful and unclean?

2. Are babies born bad?

3. What is original sin?

4. What constitutes sin?

5. Is there a difference between Sin and sins?

6. What does sin do to divine and human relationships?

7. In light of humanity's plight, what is our most basic and desperate need?

Analogies Of Redemption

By the cross of Christ, we have been redeemed. Now we are reconciled to God. Once we were enemies, but now we are friends of God. Our sins have been forgiven and forgotten. We were made children of God by pure grace. How did this happen? How did the cross and the empty tomb bring us redemption and release? Though we cannot fully explain the "how" of redemption, the New Testament gives us several analogies to help us understand. Which of these analogies speaks best to you? Check your answer:

1. ___ Courtroom. You are a criminal. God the Father is the judge. You plead guilty. The sentence is death. But Christ is your advocate and he takes the punishment in your behalf so that you go free.

2. ___ Altar. Christ is the lamb that is sacrificed for your sins. He is both priest and the victim to be offered. He offers himself as a sacrifice for the sin of the world. "Behold the lamb of God who takes away the sin of the world." Our sins are put upon him and he carries them to his death. Jesus' death was vicarious and substitutionary.

3. ___ Slave market. All of us are slaves of sin and Satan. Christ comes to the slave market and buys us out of slavery. The price is his own precious blood. We were bought with a price. Now we belong to him and we are his slaves. To be his slave is perfect freedom.

4. ___ Victory in war. There is a war going on between God and Satan. The battlefield is the cross. God uses Jesus as bait to catch the devil. By the cross he is caught and defeated. The strife is over; the battle is won. Satan's doom is sealed and Christ and his people are victors over sin, death, and hell.

135

Lord Of All?

To what extent is Jesus "Lord" of our lives? Does he hold absolute sway over every area of our lives? Suppose we look at our lives as a wheel with Jesus as the hub. In how many areas of your life does Jesus dominate?

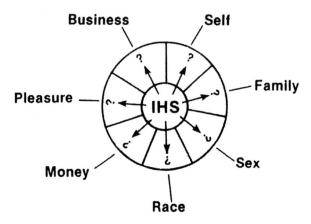

A Summary

Martin Luther in his *Small Catechism* summed up all we have been studying in this chapter. It is worthy of memorization. Please turn to his summary on page 132. He answers the following questions. Can you find the answers? If not, ask help from your fellow students.

1. Who is Jesus?

2. What did Jesus do for me?

3. Who am I?

4. How did Jesus redeem me?

5. Why did Jesus redeem me?

God The Holy Spirit

The Third Article Of The Apostles' Creed

Traditional Version

"I believe in the Holy Ghost; the holy catholic church, the communion of saints; the forgiveness of sins; the resurrection of the body, and the life everlasting."

Ecumenical Version

"I believe in the Holy Spirit, the holy catholic church, the communion of saints, the forgiveness of sins, the resurrection of the body, and the life everlasting."

Chapter 10

The Christian's Unknown God

Like the Greeks of Saint Paul's day, Christians today have an unknown God. In a sermon preached in Athens, Paul called attention to an altar he saw with the inscription "To an unknown god" (Acts 17:23). If Paul could preach to our generation, he would probably identify this unknown god as the Holy Spirit. He would find many in today's church like those he found in Ephesus. When he asked the people whether they received the Holy Spirit, they replied, "No, we have never heard that there is a Holy Spirit."

The Holy Spirit is clouded with mystery. We do not know whether we should refer to the Spirit as "he," "she," or "it." For many the Spirit is a ghost: "Holy Ghost." It is not only mysterious but scary. It is a mystery whether or not we have the Spirit. Do we have the Spirit? We really don't know. If we do have the Spirit, what kind of spirit do we have? Everyone has a spirit; otherwise we would be dead. Do we have a good or bad, a holy or an unholy spirit? Before we can answer, we must get to know the Holy Spirit. How can we say in the Apostles' Creed, "I believe in the Holy Spirit," if we do not know the Spirit?

What is the subject of the third paragraph of the creed? Does it consist of one or several subjects? Is it about the Spirit only or is it about other subjects: church, saints, forgiveness, resurrection, and everlasting life? In the first paragraph of the creed, we have God the Father; in the second, we have God the Son — no other subject than the Father and the Son. Since the creed is based upon the Trinity, the third article deals with God the Holy Spirit. It is the Spirit that produces the church, the saints, forgiveness of sins, resurrection of the body, and life everlasting. The Holy Spirit can be compared to an antenna which has extensions. See the following diagram:

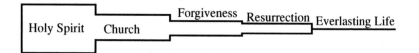

Holy Spirit | Church | Forgiveness | Resurrection | Everlasting Life

Consider now the relation of the Spirit to the Trinity. With the three articles in place, we have the answer to the basic question, "Who am I?" By virtue of God the Father's creation, I am a creature of God. "I am fearfully and wonderfully made" (Psalm 139:14). Because of the work of redemption by God the Son, I am a child of God. I have been redeemed and accepted by virtue of Christ's sacrificial death on the cross. "But to all who received him, who believed in his name, he gave power to become children of God" (John 1:12). By the spirit's work of sanctification, I am *becoming what I am.* Why am I becoming a child of God? In essence I am a child of God by grace through faith but in practice I do not live like one. This means I am at the same time a saint and a sinner, *simul iustis et peccator.* I have a dual nature. There is a conflict between what I am and what I ought to be. In Romans 7:15-25 Paul describes this conflict in himself. It means that the Christian life is a process of growth. We are saved but, as Paul wrote, we must work out our salvation (Philippians 2:12). How then do I become what I am? It is by the possession of the Holy Spirit and allowing the Spirit to work in you.

The Spirit Is God

Who is the Holy Spirit? He is God, the third person of the Trinity. Jesus told the Samaritan woman at the well, "God is spirit" (John 4:24). Since God is spirit, the Holy Spirit is God. The Athanasian Creed puts it simply: "The Father is God; the Son is God; and the Holy Spirit is God." Since the Spirit is God, we refer to the Spirit as "He."

What is the meaning of "spirit"? The word for "spirit" in Hebrew is *ruach*, in Greek it is *pneuma*, in Latin *spiritus*, in German *geist*. In all these languages the word means "breath" or "wind." In his conversation with Nicodemus, Jesus referred to the Spirit as "wind" (John 3:8). One time a father helped his little boy launch a kite. As soon as the boy got the kite up, the wind died down. "Oh, please, dear God," he prayed, "no matter what you do, don't stop breathing now."

The Spirit is associated with breathing. Since God is Spirit, he breathed into Adam and he became a living being (Genesis 2:7). He was made in "the image of God," meaning he was like God in that he had a spiritual quality, a soul. Likewise, on Easter night Jesus gave the disciples the Spirit when "he breathed on them" (John 20:22).

What does it mean then to possess the Holy Spirit? To have the Spirit is to have:

- God the Father — "God is Spirit" (John 4:24).
- God the Son — "The Lord is the Spirit" (2 Corinthians 3:17).
- Life — "The Spirit gives life" (John 6:63).
- Love — "The fruit of the Spirit is love ..." (Galatians 5:22).
- Power — "You shall receive power when the Holy Spirit comes upon you" (Acts 1:8).
- Wisdom — "To one is given through the Spirit the utterance of wisdom" (1 Corinthians 12:8).
- New creation — "So if anyone is in Christ, there is a new creation" (2 Corinthians 5:17).

A Personal God

A common mistake in thinking about the Holy Spirit is to think of him in impersonal terms. This is expressed when we refer to him as "It." The Spirit is not an idea, ideal, or a principle. He is a person, the third person of the Trinity. As a person he has his own individuality along with the Father and the Son. In his final discourse with the disciples, Jesus promised to send them "another counselor" (John 14:16). The Greek word for "another" is not *heteros,* meaning different as in "heterosexual," but *allos,* meaning the "same." The promised Spirit is not another or different person from Jesus. He would come to them in terms of the Spirit. To have the Holy Spirit is to have Christ. As Paul says, "God has sent the Spirit of his Son into our hearts, crying 'Abba! Father!' "

The Holy Spirit is a person who dwells in persons. The area of God the Father is the universe: invisible, infinite, and incomprehensible. The area of God the Son is Jesus of Nazareth in whom the Spirit fully dwelt. The area of God the Spirit is the believer. Paul asks, "Do you not know that you are God's temple and that God's Spirit dwells in you?" (1 Corinthians 3:16). Here we have the immanence of God. God the Spirit is in our hearts. He is an internal reality, a personal possession. In Jesus God is *with* us. In the Holy Spirit, God is *in* us. To have God in us, we must have the Holy Spirit. Do we? When did we receive the Holy Spirit? How does the Spirit come to a believer?

How To Get The Holy Spirit

Is the Holy Spirit a natural endowment? Do we have the Spirit by virtue of our creation? One of today's heresies is the belief that God is born in you because you are a human. Shirley MacLaine of the New Age says, "Anybody can find God by getting in touch with the inner self." In a letter to me from a woman: "People don't go to church to find or see God *per se*, but to share the God within themselves with others." A student says, "I was converted three weeks ago and I received the Holy Spirit yesterday." A pastor reports, "Six people were converted to Christ in our church last Sunday, and two others received the Holy Spirit." A rancher confesses, "Now that I am a Christian, I'm praying that he will give me his Holy Spirit." What is wrong about the above statements? The Spirit does not necessarily come from an intense emotional experience. It is not required that one roll on the floor, froth at the mouth, hear angels sing or bells ring. The Spirit usually comes regularly and quietly without fanfare when he comes in his Word.

The Holy Spirit comes to us in and through the Word of God contained in the scriptures. The Spirit and the Word are inseparable. The Word is like a wet sponge. Touch or squeeze it and water is felt. Squeeze the sponge of the Word and the Spirit is received. In Ephesians Paul urges us to take "the sword of the Spirit which is the Word of God." Martin Luther agreed with Paul: "For God will not give you his Spirit without the external Word." In the Augsburg Confession, the church affirmed this truth: "For through Word and Sacraments, as through instruments, the Holy Spirit is given, and the Holy Spirit produces faith, where and when it pleases

God, in those who hear the gospel." Paul makes the Spirit and the Word synonymous. He writes, "Be filled with the *Spirit*" (Ephesians 5:18), and again, "Let the *word* of Christ dwell in you richly" (Colossians 3:16).

How does the Word come that we may receive the Spirit? First, there is the audible Word. We receive the Spirit when the oral Word is heard in preaching, teaching, and witnessing. The Spirit came to Cornelius and his group while Peter preached the Word (Acts 10:44). This is at least one very good reason for going to worship: to hear the Word proclaimed.

Second, there is the legible Word. The Spirit can come to one who is reading the Word in the Bible. In the quiet of his garden, Augustine heard a voice saying, *"Teke, lege,"* "Take, read." He opened his Bible and read, "Put on the Lord Jesus Christ" (Romans 13:14). The Spirit came and called him to faith. It changed his life from a profligate to a prophet. It still can happen to Bible readers today.

Third, there is the visible Word. The Word comes in and through the Sacraments, Baptism, and Holy Communion. This is possible because a sacrament is the Word accompanied by an external sign such as water and wine. At his baptism, Jesus received the Holy Spirit symbolized by the descending dove. Jesus instructed Nicodemus that "you must be born from above" (John 3:7). A Christian is a twice-born person, physically and spiritually. The spiritual birth takes place at baptism. On Pentecost Peter told the new believers to repent and be baptized to receive the Holy Spirit. When infants or adults are baptized, they receive the Spirit. Likewise, in Holy Communion the Spirit is renewed with fresh outpourings of the Spirit. The Word in the Lord's Supper is Christ who comes in the forms of bread and wine.

Fourth, there is the physical Word. The Spirit comes with the laying on of hands. The hands seem to be the physical connection or conductor for the Spirit to come from God to the believer. The people in Samaria received the Spirit when the apostles laid their hands on them (Acts 8:17). Today the church practices the laying on of hands for the Spirit to come. In baptism, the pastor's hands are placed on the head of a confirmand while he says, "The Father in heaven, for Jesus' sake, renew and increase in you the gift of the Holy Spirit." When a minister is ordained into the gospel ministry, a bishop lays his hands on the head of the ordinand for the gift of the Spirit and for the setting apart to preach the Word and administer the sacraments.

It is clear from the above that the Holy Spirit is a gift of God and not human achievement. The Spirit cannot be earned nor bought at any price. In the days of the apostles, Simon learned that lesson. Read about it: Acts 8:18-24.

Do you have the Holy Spirit? How can you be sure you do? There are several signs that the Holy Spirit possesses a person. Do you have faith in Christ? It is a gift of the Spirit. Do you belong to a church? The Holy Spirit brought you into the fellowship. Do you love God and your neighbor? Love is the greatest fruit of the Spirit.

Keeping The Spirit

Once having the Spirit does not mean always having the Spirit. The Spirit may not only come but go from us. In the Church of the Redeemer, Atlanta, there is a baptismal font with an elaborate font cover consisting of hand-carved woodwork in which there is a dove to symbolize the Holy Spirit received at baptism. The only mistake in the symbolism of the entire church is that the dove is shown ascending rather than descending. At baptism, the Spirit is to come down, not up. Yet, there is a lesson in the mistake: the Spirit can leave a person.

When Samson's hair was cut, "He did not know that the Lord [Spirit] had left him" (Judges 16:20). The Spirit can leave us when we, like Samson, break our relationship with him. Samson's long hair was a symbol of the covenant he had with God. The cutting of the hair was the breaking of the relationship, and as a result the Spirit left him.

We are ever in danger of losing the Spirit. We can resist the Holy Spirit as the persecutors of Stephen did (Acts 7:51). The consequence was the martyrdom of Stephen. Also, we can lie to the Spirit as Ananias and Sapphira did, when they kept back money from the sale of their property. In this case, lying to the Spirit resulted in the death of the couple. Moreover, we are not to grieve

144

the Holy Spirit by indulging in wickedness (Ephesians 4:30). It is possible to quench, to kill the Spirit (1 Thessalonians 5:19). Whatever we do against the Spirit constitutes the unpardonable sin (Matthew 12:31-32). Since the Spirit convinces us of sin, calls us to believe, and draws us to Christ, opposition to the Spirit results in our not coming to Christ for forgiveness. If any person worries if he/she has committed the unpardonable sin, he/she can be assured that if the question is asked, the sin has not been committed. The person who sins against the Holy Spirit is not concerned about sin.

How does one lose the Spirit? It is by neglect of receiving the Word of God. If Bible reading, worship, prayer, and Christian fellowship are neglected, the Spirit is probably on the way out of your life. The reception of the Spirit is not a one-time experience. A person is never "full of the Spirit." The Spirit needs to be renewed and replenished every time the Word is proclaimed and received.

The Christian's Unknown God

Try This For Thought
Consider the following questions for individual or group discussion:

1. Does the Holy Spirit come with a second blessing?

2. Is the coming of the Holy Spirit the second coming of Christ?

3. Can one get the Holy Spirit without a Pentecost experience?

4. To be a genuine Christian, must one speak in tongues?

5. Did the Holy Spirit originate on Pentecost?

6. Can one have the Holy Spirit without being a Charismatic?

7. How can one be sure he/she has the Holy Spirit?

8. Who or what is the Holy Spirit?

9. What is the work of the Holy Spirit?

10. Is it wrong to be baptized a second time?

Who Is The Spirit?
Fill in the blanks below by reading the Bible reference:
1. The Spirit is _____. (Leviticus 11:44)
2. The Spirit is the spirit of _____. (2 Corinthians 3:17)
3. The Spirit is _____. (John 6:63)
5. The Spirit is _____. (Acts 1:8)

Where Does The Spirit Dwell?

God the Father dwells in the universe. God the Son dwells in Jesus of Nazareth. Where does the Spirit dwell? Which of the following statements are true or false? Circle your answer:

T   F   1. The Holy Spirit is the possession of all people.
T   F   2. The Holy Spirit is possessed by believers in Christ.
T   F   3. The Spirit comes naturally when we are physically born.
T   F   4. The Spirit causes a person to be born anew.
T   F   5. Repentance and faith are preconditions to possessing the Spirit.

Do You Have The Holy Spirit?

To test whether or not you have the Spirit, check the following evidence of the Spirit.

1. ___ Have you been baptized?
2. ___ Do you have faith to say Jesus is your Lord?
3. ___ Are you an active member of a church?
4. ___ Do you love God and people?
5. ___ Do you witness for Jesus Christ?

Coming And Going

The Holy Spirit comes and goes. Is it possible for the Spirit to leave and us not to know it? Read about Samson (Judges 16:20).

What can cause the going of the Spirit from us?

1. Resist — Read Acts 7:51.

2. Lie to the Holy Spirit — Read Acts 5:3.

3. Grieve the Holy Spirit — Read Ephesians 4:30.

4. Quench the Spirit — Read 1 Thessalonians 5:19.

5. Commit the unpardonable sin — Read Matthew 12:31-32.

Chapter 11

The Spirit And The Church

When we say in the Apostles' Creed, "I believe in the Holy Spirit," we confess our faith in "the holy catholic church, the communion of saints." This causes us to ask what the church is and what the Spirit has to do with her.

What is the church? In a sense, she is a physical building, but she is more than that! She is a hierarchy of leaders consisting of pastors, bishops, cardinals, and a pope. But the church is more than that! She is more than a liturgy with various forms of worship. She may be considered a creed with systematic beliefs, but she is more than that. The creed tells us what the church is: "the holy catholic church, the communion of saints." In this last phrase, the comma stands for the word "is." Thus we are saying, "the holy catholic church *is* the communion of saints."

The church, then, consists of saints. Frequently the New Testament refers to church members as "saints." The word is used not in the moral but in the religious sense. Saints are forgiven believers. In God's sight believers are saints because they wear the perfect robe of Christ's righteousness. God, therefore, pronounced them perfect, for he sees them clothed in Christ's righteousness. God, therefore, pronounced them perfect, for he sees them clothed in Christ's perfection. In actuality, church people are saints in pursuit of sanctification, in becoming saintly saints.

Saints are church people. The church consists of God's people who have entered a covenant with God through Christ. We belong to God's family, because through baptism God has adopted us as his children. Peter described the church as "a chosen race, a royal priesthood, a holy nation, God's own people" (1 Peter 2:9). Repeatedly Paul refers to the church as the body of Christ (Colossians 1:24). Believers are members of his body. The church is the body of Christ, and the people of the church make up the body with

Christ as the head of the body. Often the church is described as "the contemporary incarnation of Christ."

The church, then, consists of people who are at the same time both sinners and saints. The church is not a museum of perfect people but a hospital of sick sinners. This means that no one is too good to stay out and no one is too bad to come in. Hence, the church has her weaknesses, limitations, and sins. The church is what we are. It consists of many who are halfhearted, doubtful, inactive, insensitive, and often immoral. Among the charges are sexual abuse, embezzlement, and infidelity. If anyone is looking for a perfect church to join, don't join, because as a sinner you would ruin it! It is a sign of God's amazing grace that the church continues to exist, grow, and serve in spite of her imperfect members.

The Fellowship Of The Church

The creed further defines the church as the "communion of saints." The church is a community of faith. "Communion" means "fellowship." Christianity is not an individualist or solitary religion. A true Christian cannot be independent of other Christians. The church consists of believers in Jesus as the Christ according to Peter's confession at Caesarea Philippi. The first Christians had this commonality: "And all who believed were together and had all things in common" (Acts 2:44).

What kind of fellowship is the church?

1. The church is a *believing* fellowship. She consists of those who say together the Apostles' Creed. The people of the church are unanimous in believing that Jesus is Lord and Savior.

2. The church is a *redemptive* fellowship. The members have been redeemed by Christ's sacrifice on the cross from sin, death, and hell. Church people become redeemed by accepting Christ. The church is the society of the saved.

3. The church is a *worshiping* fellowship. On the first day of the week for twenty centuries members of the church gathered to thank and praise God for his blessings. They come to hear the Word of God taught and preached. Then they go out to bear witness to the truth they heard and to serve in Christ's name. Mother Teresa

was an example of one who served Christ by serving the poorest of the poor.

The church is a *serving* fellowship. As Jesus came to serve, his followers gathered in the church are dedicated and committed to sharing God's love to the poor and helpless. They do it for Jesus' sake.

The Creator Of The Christian Church

Who founded the church? Jesus? Surely he laid the foundation for it by his cross and empty tomb. But the birthday of the church is not Good Friday nor Easter. Pentecost is the birthday of the church, because then the Holy Spirit came to the disciples. For the first time the gospel was preached and the sacrament of baptism was administered. It was on Pentecost that the Spirit caused 3,000 to respond by confessing Jesus as Lord. The church, therefore, is a divine creation born of the Holy Spirit. No human founds a church, but the Spirit working through humans gives birth to the church.

As we have already seen, the church consists of individual Christians. They constitute a fellowship of faith in Christ. Obviously, there can be no church without individual Christians. Therefore, the Spirit, to found the church, must make individual Christians. And so he does! A hymn says, "I was made a Christian." The Spirit brought each of us into the church through a new birth. But how does the Spirit make a Christian out of a pagan?

First, the Spirit *calls* us. As a person, I do not decide to be a follower of Christ. It is God's Spirit who calls and chooses me to be a disciple. I do not seek God, but Christ, the Good Shepherd, seeks and finds me. A few years ago an evangelist popularized the phrase, "I found it!" The truth is we do not find God or salvation, but he finds us. Jesus said, "No one can come to me unless the Father who sent me draws him" (John 6:44). Paul found this to be true: "No one can say 'Jesus is Lord' except by the Holy Spirit." Moreover, faith in Christ is a gift of the Spirit. Paul taught: "To another faith by the same Spirit" (1 Corinthians 12:9). One of the nine fruits of the Spirit is faith (Galatians 5:22). "Faith comes from what is heard, and what is heard comes by the preaching of Christ"

(Romans 10:17). The Spirit comes in the Word so that as the Word is heard, the Spirit creates faith.

Christians are a called and chosen people. Each person is called to be a Christian rather than deciding by one's own desire and will that it would be a good thing to be a Christian. In the explanation of the third article of the Creed, Luther said, "I cannot by my own reason or strength believe in Jesus or come to him, but the Holy Spirit has called me through the gospel...." It is the highest honor that God, through the Spirit, calls a person to be his child. Several people were once discussing who was a VIP. One said that a VIP was one who was invited to the White House for a conference with the President. A second person said that a VIP was one invited to the White House for a conference with the President, and when the phone rang, the president did not answer it to avoid interrupting the conference. The third person said, "No, a VIP is one invited to the White House for a conference with the President, the phone rang, the president answered it, and handed it to the VIP and said, 'It is for you.' " Likewise, God makes a personal call to each of us to belong to him and join his church. The call comes through the gospel when it is read, taught, or preached.

Does this call come to only certain ones? Are some predestined or elected to be saved and others not? God calls every human to come to him. In John 3:16 Jesus says, "*Whoever* believes in him may not perish but may have everlasting life." God does not desire anyone to perish, die, or go to hell. To prevent this, he gave his only Son to die for us. However, a human response to God's call is necessary for salvation. When God calls, we must answer: "Here am I." We answer in terms of faith and obedience.

Second, we are made Christians by the Spirit's *convicting* us. When the Spirit comes, we are convicted and convinced of sin, righteousness, and judgment (John 16:8). Jesus taught that the Spirit would lead and guide us into truth. In other words, the Spirit opens our eyes. He enlightens us to see what we never saw before. There is a story about a boy carrying a basket with a sign on it, "Heathen Puppies." Inside were three tiny, newborn puppies. A week later he went down the street again with the basket, but this time the sign said, "Christian Puppies." Someone asked him how come they were now Christian puppies. He explained, "Now they have their eyes open."

The Holy Spirit opens our eyes to see ourselves as sinners in need of Christ. Moreover, he enables us to see that Jesus is the Christ. The Spirit gave Peter at Caesarea Philippi the insight to declare that Jesus is the Christ. The Spirit gave Simeon the ability to recognize the Messiah in the forty-day-old Jesus when he was presented in the temple. Because of the Spirit, we understand spiritual realities formerly hidden and not understood. This understanding leads to our acceptance of Christ as our Lord and Savior.

Third, the Spirit makes us Christians by *converting* us. When the Spirit comes to us through the Word, we receive the Holy Spirit. He causes us to be born from above, as Jesus told Nicodemus (John 3:5). The Spirit creates in us a new heart from which flows a good life. "I will give them one heart, and put a new spirit within them; I will take the stony heart out of their flesh and give them a heart of flesh, that they may walk in my statutes and keep my ordinances and obey them" (Ezekiel 11:19-20). The new heart is filled with God's Spirit who changes a person from evil to good. This was demonstrated in King Saul to whom the prophet Samuel said, "Then the Spirit of the Lord will come mightily upon you, and you shall prophesy with them and be *turned into another man.*"

How can I live the Christian life? How can I be as good as God expects me to be? Is it possible to be as holy as God is holy? The answer to these questions is the Holy Spirit. He is the power to change, to transform, and to make us good and to do good. Thus, the work of the Holy Spirit is sanctification, derived from the Latin word meaning "holy." If we have the Holy Spirit, we will become holy.

Living the godly life, therefore, is an internal matter. It deals with the heart and the spirit in the heart. Out of the heart flows either good or bad words and deeds. God's Spirit produces moral fruit in us. Paul lists them in Galatians 5:22: "Love, joy, peace, patience, kindness, goodness, faithfulness, gentleness, and self-control." Would you not agree that anyone having these nine virtues would be a good, godly, holy person? The important thing to notice, however, is that the Holy Spirit does this in and through us. The good life does not result from the force of discipline imposed from without, nor from rules and regulations, nor from following a book of discipline, nor from the imperatives "must" and "ought." Paul speaks of these virtues as fruit. Jesus taught that a good tree produces good fruit. Our problem is being a good tree. A good person does good deeds. Good deeds do not make a good person.

It is to be noted also in this analogy of fruit that the fruit comes naturally. If the tree is good, the fruit is good. Have you ever seen a tree fret or worry over whether or not the fruit would be good? Does a tree strain and try and try to produce fruit? No, fruit comes naturally, normally, spontaneously. So it is with living the Christian life. Virtues come naturally from a heart filled with the Spirit. Therefore, we should not try to do better or make ourselves do good things. That kind of living makes nervous saints. There is no joy in this kind of life. Rather, our concern should be to have more and more of the Spirit. To get him means to spend more time with the Word as it is read, taught, and preached.

Fourth, the Spirit makes us Christians in daily living by giving us *confirmation* that we are God's people. Are you saved? Are you going to heaven? Many answer with some doubt: "I hope I am," or "I would like to go to heaven." Can we Christians be sure we belong to God? Can we be certain of our eternal destiny? What guarantee or assurance do we have, if any?

The Holy Spirit is our assurance that we are God's children. Hear Paul: "When we cry, 'Abba! Father!' it is the Spirit himself bearing witness with our spirit that we are children of God" (Romans 8:16). According to Paul, the Spirit in our hearts serves as a guarantee that we are saved, that we are forgiven, and that we are going to heaven. In Ephesians he writes, "sealed with the promised Holy Spirit, which is the guarantee of our inheritance" (1:13-14). Often the Spirit is referred to as "earnest." It refers to a real estate deal. The buyer puts up earnest money as assurance of final payment and possession of the property. Having the Spirit is the earnest money which guarantees our ultimate inheritance in heaven. The Spirit is also described as a seal. The seal is a mark of certainty and authority. Our relationship with God is sealed by the Spirit received at baptism. Because we have the Spirit, we can be absolutely certain that we are God's children, that we are redeemed and bound for heaven.

The Gathering Agent
Even though the Holy Spirit made individual Christians, the church does not yet exist. It is not a church until the individuals are brought into a fellowship, "the communion of saints." What or who will gather them into one body, the church?

The gathering agent is the Holy Spirit. He attracts and draws the individuals into a oneness with Christ and each other. The Spirit is a centripetal force that draws, binds, and cements into oneness. In the diagram below is the independent status before the work of the Spirit. After the Spirit, the individuals constitute the church.

Before The Spirit Gathers

Christian   Christian   Christian

Christian   Christian

Christian

After The Spirit Gathers

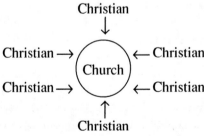

When the Spirit exists in a church, there is unity. When an evil spirit, the devil, gets into a church, there are schisms, factions, controversy, and divisions. We need to be aware that the unholy as well as the Holy Spirit can dwell in a church. When Peter tried to persuade Jesus not to go to Jerusalem to die, Jesus recognized that Satan was speaking through Peter. Regretfully some times church members may be agents of Satan. Some years ago, a businessman bought a downtown African-American church to extend his property for his expanding business. The church agreed to sell, the money was paid, but when the time came for the church to vacate, the congregation failed to move. The purchaser did not want to take the church to court. He decided upon a plan to scare them off. At an evening service, he had the main power switch turned off, had a car's headlights focused on the window over the altar, and then in a devil suit climbed through the window for all to see him. The people, scared of the devil, rushed to the exits. All got out except one elderly lady in a wheelchair. As the "devil" got close to her, she excitedly said, "Now listen here, Satan. I have been in this church all my life. I taught Sunday School for fifty years, and I have been president of the Women's Society for 25 years. And I want you to know I have been on your side all the time!"

The Holy Spirit gathers individuals into a church. What does it mean to join a church? One Sunday morning a pastor invited children to come forward for a sermonette. A dialogue between the pastor and the children went like this: "If you girls joined the Boy Scouts, would you be boys? No! If you boys joined the Girl Scouts would you be girls? No! If you joined the Elks Club, would you be Elks, or a Lions Club, or a Moose Club?" Each time the answer was "No." Then he asked, "If you joined the church, would you be Christians?" He answered, "NO!"

The pastor's answer apparently showed that he did not understand the work of the Spirit, the nature of the church, or the meaning of church membership. What is the church? Is it only something like a civic club? It is the body of Christ, God's people, the society of the saved. To belong to the church is to belong to God's Kingdom. To join the church is to become a Christian.

What is the meaning of church membership? How does one become a member? One joins the church through baptism, which is a covenant between God and a repentant and believing person. Baptism is the incorporation into the corpus (body) of Christ. God adopts us as his children and automatically we become members of his family in the church. At baptism, as in the case of Jesus' baptism, the Holy Spirit is received and a new birth takes place. To be in Christ is to be in the church.

If repentance and faith are necessary for baptism, it is not possible for one to be baptized. The one to be baptized must respond to God's call through the Spirit in terms of repentance and faith. To be certain that these conditions exist, the church asks candidates for baptism to take instruction when the meaning of baptism is explained.

Gifts Of The Spirit

Just as the Holy Spirit produces a ninefold fruit of virtue in the individual, the Spirit provides a ninefold gift to the church for her to carry out her mission in the world. In 1 Corinthians 12, Paul lists the gifts: wisdom, knowledge, faith, healing, miracles, interpretation of tongues, prophecy, distinguishing between spirits, and speaking in tongues. These gifts to the church have certain characteristics:

- They are gifts of the Spirit and not human attainment.
- Every member of the church has at least one of these gifts.
- Each person does not necessarily have all nine gifts.
- A gift is given according to the specific need at a given time.
- The gifts are not of equal value nor importance. The most important is love (1 Corinthians 13:13) and the least important is speaking in tongues (1 Corinthians 14:19).

Probably the most controversial of the gifts is the speaking in tongues. Of the thirty million charismatics in America, five million claim they speak in tongues. The problem resulting from those speaking in tongues is division in the church. Some divide the church into first- and second-class Christians depending on the ability to speak in tongues. Tongue-speaking Christians claim that the ability to speak in tongues proves that a person is a complete Christian.

In chapter 14 of 1 Corinthians, Saint Paul compares two kinds of Christian speaking:

Tongues	Preaching
Speaks to God (v. 2)	Speaks to the church
Edifies only the speaker (v. 4)	Edifies the church (v. 3)

Less than the preacher (v. 5)	Greater than the speaker in tongues (v. 5)
Unintelligible (v. 9)	Intelligible
Building up of speaker	Building up of church (v. 12)
Pray with the spirit (v. 14)	Pray with mind (vv. 14, 19)
For believers (v. 23)	For unbelievers (vv. 24, 25)

The Church And Churches

By the year 2000 it is estimated that there will be about two billion members of the church divided among 1,600 denominations in America and 23,500 in the world. Which of these many churches is the one true church? Is there only one true church or are all of them true churches? Are churches true churches that claim to be churches? Are the Church of the Latter Day Saints; the Church of Christ, Scientist; the Church of Scientology; or the Unification Church true churches? Can every church advertise as one did: "We are the only church authorized to preach Jesus Christ"?

What does the Apostles' Creed say about the true church? It asserts that we believe in "the holy catholic church." It is "the" and not "a" church. The church we believe in is not one of many churches, but the one and only church. There is not a church of Peter, of Paul, or Luther or Calvin or Wesley. The church of Jesus Christ is one church. We belong to the Christian church whether it is Eastern Orthodox, Roman Catholic, or Protestant.

Moreover, the creed says that the church is "holy." How can it be holy when it is composed of sinners? The church is holy because it is the product of the Holy Spirit. The Spirit dwells in and works through the church. The church is the custodian of the holy Bible and administers the holy sacraments. The people in the church are God's holy people, because their bodies are temples of the Spirit. In the church God comes to meet his people assembled for worship and service.

Added to this, the church is "catholic." "I believe in the holy catholic church." Often Protestants ask why Protestants say they believe in the "catholic" church. The word "catholic" is spelled with a small "c." If it were a large "C," it would refer to the Roman Catholic Church. Spelled with a small "c," the word means orthodox, universal, or ecumenical. The word "catholic" means to say that the church is for all people everywhere. It has no geographical, social, racial, or national boundaries. It is not the church *of* America but the church *in* America. The church belongs to nobody but Jesus Christ.

The implication of "catholic" is that all Christians are one in Christ regardless of denomination. On the night before his death, Jesus prayed "that they may be one" (John 17:11). This is not a reality at the present time but we are making progress toward it. In 1997 Evangelical Lutherans, Presbyterians, Reformed, and United Church of Christ adopted a manifesto declaring altar and pulpit fellowship. This means members of these churches welcome members of the above churches for Holy Communion and it means the pastors may serve in these churches as pastors. Soon it is expected that Evangelical Lutherans and Episcopalians will sign a similar agreement. Denominationalism is on the decrease. Many do not join a church on the basis of the denominational name but because the church meets their spiritual needs. In 1997 Evangelical Lutherans and Roman Catholics made a historic joint declaration. It was the first joint declaration made by Roman Catholics with a church of the Reformation. The key segment of the document says, "Together we confess: By grace alone, in faith in Christ's saving work and not because of any merit on our part, we are accepted by God and receive the Holy Spirit, who renews our hearts while equipping and calling us to good works." After an interdenominational service, a Roman Catholic priest's car refused to start. People passing by saw the priest, an Episcopal and a Congregational minister pushing the old car along the street. "This," explained a vicar, "is called an ecumenical movement!"

The Church's Reason For Existence

In recent years many churches have produced a mission statement publicized in their literature and banners. The statement is to tell the world why she exists. Why did the Holy Spirit create the church? Is the church relevant to the twenty-first century and does it have a future or is it a fossil of a past age? The New Testament tells the purpose of the church in certain Greek words.

1. *Leitourgia*. The word "liturgy" comes from this word. One purpose of the church is to worship the triune God. The church is a

worshiping community. Each Sunday approximately fifty million people are in church glorifying God and listening to his Word.

2. *Kerygma.* The word means "proclamation." The church exists to proclaim the gospel to the world. Accordingly, the church supports and conducts evangelism and missions throughout the world. Its goal is to make disciples of all nations.

3. *Didache.* The word refers to the teaching ministry of the church. The church exists to teach the truth of God's Word. The Bible is explained. Doctrines are discussed. In his final words to his disciples, he said, "... teaching them to obey...."

4. *Koinonia. Koinonia* means fellowship. The church is a community of faith. People share their faith and experiences. It is a fellowship of love for each other. They work together to serve the Lord.

5. *Marturia.* The Greek word means "witness." The word "martyr" comes from it. The first Christian martyr was Stephen, who was stoned to death for his witness to Christ as Lord. Each member of the church has the privilege of sharing the faith with others.

6. *Diaconia.* The church exists to serve as Jesus said, "The Son of Man came not to be served but to serve." From this word came the words "deacon" and "deaconess." They are rendering service. Each member of the church has the privilege and responsibility to help, share, and care for people in need.

Here are six excellent reasons for the church's existence. Is your congregation fulfilling these reasons?

The Spirit And The Church

The Paradox Of A Christian

The work of God the Spirit is sanctification. If by faith in Christ, Christians are God's people, why is sanctification needed? It is due to the dual and duel nature of a Christian. A Christian has a dual nature because a Christian is a saint and sinner at the same time. He/she has a duel nature because the two natures are in constant conflict. See Romans 7:21-25.

What does Ephesians say we are? _____

What does 1 John 1:8 say we are? _____

Put the following under the proper heading: Justification, Sanctification, Being a Christian, Becoming a Christian, What God did for us, What God does in us, Saved, Being Saved.

Saint	**Sinner**
1.	1.
2.	2.
3.	3.
4.	4.

The Holy Catholic Church

This phrase tells us what kind of church the Spirit creates.
1. What is "holy" about your church? Check your answers.
　　____ a. Members are pious.
　　____ b. Members have the Holy Spirit.
　　____ c. Members are sinless.
　　____ d. Members do good works.

161

___ e. The church has the holy Bible.

___ f. The Sacraments are holy.

___ g. The holy presence of Christ.

2. Why do Protestants say they believe in the "catholic" church? What does "catholic" mean? Check your answer:

    ___ a. Roman Catholic Church.

    ___ b. Eastern Orthodox Church.

    ___ c. Protestant Church.

    ___ d. Church of the white race only.

    ___ e. Church of a nation.

    ___ f. Universal, worldwide, ecumenical.

The Communion Of Saints

The creed defines the church as the "communion of saints." What is a saint? Answer Yes or No:

1. ___ A saint is a morally perfect person.

2. ___ A saint is one pronounced a saint by the church.

3. ___ A saint is a super-Christian now in heaven.

4. ___ A saint is a believer in Christ.

4. ___ A saint is a person justified by grace.

6. ___ A saint is a forgiven sinner.

What Is Your Answer?

1. Can one be a church member and not a Christian?

2. Can one be a Christian and not be a member of the church?

3. What does it take to become a member of a church?

4. How does one become a member of a church?

5. If repentance and faith are needed, can small children belong to the church?

Gifts Of The Spirit

The Spirit gives the church various gifts for her to do her work. Read 1 Corinthians 12 to find the answers to the following questions:

1. How many gifts are listed?

2. Does a Christian have all these gifts?

3. Which is the best gift?

4. Is any Christian without at least one gift?

5. What is the purpose of the gifts?

6. Must one speak in tongues to be a true Christian?

Chapter 12

The Forgiveness Of Sins

Years ago an evangelist, Dr. Alan Walker, was walking down the center aisle of an auditorium to the stage where he was going to preach. As he walked, someone handed him a note. Backstage before the service began, he opened the note and read, "Dr. Walker, please tell us that God forgives the sin of adultery even by a foolish Christian 31 years of age."

This is the cry of Christians and non-Christians. The basic problem of the world is broken relationships. In various ways, we hurt each other and estrangement follows. We become enemies and we fight, seek revenge, and refuse to talk to each other. Indeed, it is human to err, and consequently those sins separate us from each other and from God. What can restore those relationships? The answer is in the Apostles' Creed: "the forgiveness of sins."

Some people are honest enough to say they do not believe in the forgiveness of sins. A motorcycle gang has the motto: "God forgives, Outlaws don't." In his autobiography Lee Iacocca writes, "Henry Ford made my kids suffer, and for that I'll never forgive him." Simon Wiesenthal spent many years searching for Nazi war criminals who were responsible for the holocaust. When he was a prisoner in a Nazi forced-labor camp, he was ordered to visit an SS trooper who was wounded and dying in a hospital. Knowing he was going to die, he wanted to clear his conscience by confessing his sins of shooting and burning up Jews in the Ukraine. The dying officer begged Wiesenthal, a Jew, to forgive him. Wiesenthal listened, turned, and walked away without a word in reply. After the war Wiesenthal sent the story to 32 leading religious leaders asking them whether he did the right thing. The majority agreed that he did the right thing by not forgiving the Nazi.

Though some do not forgive because they do not believe in forgiving, true Christians do believe in forgiveness. In the Apostles'

Creed they confess that they believe in "the forgiveness of sins." What does the forgiveness of sins have to do with the third article of the creed? As we learned earlier, the third article deals with the nature and work of God the Spirit. The Holy Spirit created and preserves the church, and through her the Holy Spirit offers "the forgiveness of sins, the resurrection of the body, and the life everlasting."

Our Need Of Forgiveness

If we believe in the forgiveness of sins, we automatically believe that we need to be forgiven and to forgive. We need to be forgiven because we are sinners. If we do not sin, there is no need for forgiveness. Today there is a tendency to minimize or totally deny sin. Our society has become so sinful that we take sin as the normal way of life. It is what everybody does, so it is claimed. Why then be shocked at a sin? Have you noticed that in almost every case when a criminal is indicted, he/she claims innocence? There is the usual, "I have done nothing wrong," even though the person is caught red-handed in the crime. In some cases even the church has become tolerant of sin. One of the most prominent television preachers in America says he never preaches about sin. In its worship book one of the largest Protestant denominations in America makes the confession of sins optional. Seldom from the pulpit is sin exposed and condemned. Never a word is spoken about the God of justice and his wrath against sin. All is love, love, love. But that is only half of the truth about God.

Therefore, we Christians believe that we are sinners in need of forgiveness so that we can be right with God. This need is not only for Christians but for the whole of humankind. In the early chapters of Romans, Paul concludes that "all, both Jews and Greeks, are under the power of sin," and "All have sinned and fall short of the glory of God." If you need evidence of sin in society, take a look at your daily newspaper, a tabloid of all kinds of sins.

What about Christians? Do they sin also? When Christians are baptized they receive forgiveness. Do Christians sin after baptism? In John's first letter, we read, "If we say we have no sin, we deceive ourselves, and the truth is not in us" (1 John 1:8).

166

This implies that every human being is sinful and in need of forgiveness. No person can claim innocence of wrongdoing. Every person is responsible for his/her life. We choose to sin. Like Adam and Eve we yield to temptation. We cannot dodge responsibility by blaming others, our early training, environment, genes, or whatever! Ever since Adam, we have been blaming someone or something for what we did. After God asked Adam about his sin, he explained, "This woman whom you gave to be with me, she gave me fruit from the tree and I ate" (Genesis 3:12). Sin begins in the heart that is corrupt. Therefore, we pray, "Create in me a clean heart, O God."

Is It A Sin?

What does the Bible say sin is? In the Old Testament sin is described 220 times as "iniquity," which is a distortion or perversion of what is right. Sin is considered rebellion against God leading to wickedness. "All wrongdoing is sin" (1 John 5:17). Sin is also transgression, and so we pray, "Forgive us our trespasses." We sin when we trespass on another person's person or property. As John says, "Sin is lawlessness" (1 John 3:4). This lawlessness results from disobedience to God's will and laws. The most central concept of sin in Old and New Testaments is the Greek word *Hamartia*, meaning "missing the mark." It occurs 170 times in the New Testament. To miss the mark is not to measure up to what God expects us to be and do. As the arrow fails to hit the bull's-eye, we miss the mark of holiness, purity, and righteousness. A Christian is called to be Christlike in every way: thought, word, and deed. Shortly before George Bernard Shaw died, a reporter asked him, "If you could live your life over again and be anybody you've known or any person from history, who would you be?" "I would choose," replied Shaw, "to be the man George Bernard Shaw could have been but never was." Is he not saying that his life missed the mark?

Sin then is more than a thought, word, or act. It is a condition in which we were born. We call it original sin. It is a fatal weakness in our nature that causes us to oppose God, as a rebel, and to violate his will. We come into the world under the power of sin. "In

167

sin did my mother conceive me" (Psalm 51:5). With this proclivity toward sin I cannot but sin. Sin (with a capital letter) produces sins. The cause is Sin and the fruit of Sin is sins.

Kinds Of Sins

There is a variety of sins. There are personal sins which all commit. Among these are pride, selfishness, hatred, and jealousy. Also we commit corporate sins. The church commits sin in terms of bigotry and hypocrisy. A club may indulge in sin by refusing membership to another race or religion. The state can perform horrible sins as the holocaust or in the massacre of thousands in Russia, China, Bosnia, Rwanda, and elsewhere.

In addition, there are sins of commission and omission. Both types of sin are equally serious. It is not only what we do but what we don't do. It is our refusal to help when our help is needed. The priest and the Levite in the Good Samaritan parable and the rich man, Dives, in the parable were guilty of sins of omission. It is the gift we do not give, the service we do not render, the kindness not extended. It is the sin primarily of "good" people who do nothing to resist evil. On her 75th birthday Clare Boothe Luce was asked, "Do you have any regrets?" She answered, "Yes, I should have been a better person. Kinder. More tolerant. Sometimes I wake up in the middle of the night and I remember a girlhood friend of mine who had a brain tumor and called me three times to come and see her. I was always too busy, and when she died I was profoundly ashamed. I remember that after 56 years."

And then there are sins against God and people. Little do we realize that all sins are against God. To sin against a neighbor is to sin against God. The Ten Commandments were written on two tablets of stone by God, one with our duties to God and the other with our duties to our neighbors. To kill, commit adultery, steal, lie, and covet is to break God's laws. When we cheat, lie, steal, murder, or do anything to hurt our neighbor, we sin not only against human beings but against the divine Lawgiver. When Nathan brought David's attention to his sin against Uriah and Bathsheba by murder and adultery, David confessed, "I have sinned against the Lord" (2 Samuel 12:13). How so? Didn't David sin against

168

Uriah and Bathsheba? But David rightly realized that his acts of murder and adultery were sins against Yahweh. Thus, when we break the laws of society and church, we at the same time sin against God. This means that a lawbreaker one day must give an account to God the Judge. If society fails to enact justice, there is still God's judgment to be faced. This truth implies that the laws of state and church must harmonize as far as possible with God's laws. If they do not harmonize and are opposed to God's laws, Christians have every right to disobey them, for they must obey God rather than men (Acts 5:29).

Consequences Of Sin

Sin now and pay later! In the game of life, the breaking of the rules always results in a penalty. This is illustrated in a football game. When a rule is violated, such as being offsides or grasping a face mask, the team is penalized by the loss of a certain number of yards. Break God's laws and the consequences are horrible and inescapable.

One of the penalties of sin is bondage. He who commits sin is the slave of sin. When Scrooge's partner in Dickens' *A Christmas Carol* returned from the dead, he was wrapped in chains of selfishness and stinginess. Today we call this bondage an addiction which we cannot break: smoking, drinking, drugs, sex, overeating, and so forth.

Another penalty is suffering. The sinner as well as the victim suffers. Often the victim is an innocent sufferer. Jesus is the prime example of innocent suffering at the hands of wicked men. For six years a young Chicagoan was in jail for a rape he did not commit. Only when the girl confessed that she lied was the man released.

The ultimate penalty is death. In the biblical sense, death is separation from God. And that is what hell is — separation from God. Since God is love, sin causes separation from love, and this means hatred. God is life, and to be separated from life is death. Sin breaks the relationship with God. For this reason Christ died for us that we might be reconciled with the Father. Separation from God is the human's most basic predicament, and the renewal of the relationship is the chief work of Christ.

Nothing good can be said about sin. It is always a sad story of defeat, tragedy, suffering, death, and hell. It needs to be remembered that, though we repent and are forgiven, the penalty of our sin remains, because we are not punished for our sins but by our sins. Though David was forgiven his sins of murder and adultery, he still had to pay the penalty of the loss of his child. Though the repentant thief on the cross was forgiven, the thief had to remain on the cross and die. When Pope John Paul II went to a prison in Rome to forgive his attempted assassin, Acga still had to pay the price of life in jail. Forgiveness is like pulling a nail out of a Chippendale chair. The scar remains.

The God Who Forgives

A Roman Catholic priest was teaching his congregation the new Vatican II liturgy. He explained, "When I say, 'The Lord be with you,' you respond, 'And also with you.'" The microphone he was using did not seem to be working and so he commented, "Something is wrong with this mike." Immediately the people replied, "And also with you." We have just learned that there is something wrong with everyone of us and that everything wrong we do is against God. That leads us to ask whether our God is the one who forgives.

When we confess in the Apostles' Creed that we believe in "the forgiveness of sins," we are saying that we believe in that kind of God who forgives. The Bible is full of statements that God is merciful and forgives sinners. A Psalmist sings, "For as the heavens are high above the earth, so great is his steadfast love toward those who fear him; as far as the east is from the west, so far does he remove our transgressions from us" (Psalm 103:11-12). Isaiah tells us, "Let him return to the Lord, that he may have mercy on him, and to our God, for he will abundantly pardon" (Isaiah 55:7). God's Son repeatedly forgave: "Your sins are forgiven" (Mark 2:5). The apostles preached, "If we confess our sins, he is faithful and just, and will forgive our sins and cleanse us from all unrighteousness."

Since we believe in the God who forgives, what does forgiveness mean? In the Bible, forgiveness is described and defined in various ways. When God forgives us, he hides our sins from himself so that he does not see them. Or God sends away the sins in terms of liberation from a debt. Another term for forgiveness is the blotting out of the sin by absorbing the sin and its consequences. Another way of expressing it is to wash away sins as happens in baptism. Sin may be expiated. Or it may be propitiated, covered up by the robe of Christ's righteousness. The forgiveness of God is demonstrated in Justification when, for Jesus' sake and on the basis of our faith in Jesus, the sinner is pronounced forgiven and is accepted as a child of God. Another meaningful term for forgiveness is reconciliation when there is no longer anything between God and the sinner. The gospel which the church preaches is that God is a forgiving God and that reconciliation with God is possible by faith in Christ.

Why does God forgive us? Certainly in no way do we sinners deserve forgiveness. Because of our idolatry, selfishness, and disobedience, we merit nothing but suffering, death, and hell. Why God forgives us is in his dual nature: love and justice. According to the Bible, God is love. This love prompted him to give his only Son that sinners might not perish but have everlasting life (John 3:16). In the beginning, this God of love created humans that he might have someone to love and to be loved. Sticks, stones, and stars cannot love. Thus, God made humans in his own image as spiritual beings capable of giving and receiving love. From the time of the first sin, God has been trying desperately to get people to return to him and live with him in love. Through priests, prophets, and patriarchs, God has been appealing to his people to stop sinning and return to him. In utmost desperation he sent his only Son to demonstrate, once and for all time, that he loves us. There is no greater proof of love than when one dies for another, especially when that one is not worthy to be died for. One time a stranger saved a small boy from drowning. After artificial respiration the lad came to, looked into the face of the man that saved him and said, "Thank you, sir, for saving my life." To this the man replied, "That's all right, son. Glad to do it. But see to it that you're worth saving."

God forgives also because of his nature of justice. He is a holy and just God, who cannot tolerate sin. Justice must be satisfied.

Wrongs must be righted. Sin demands death. How can a human make it up to God? There is no way! Therefore, God in his mercy decided to do for humankind what people cannot do for themselves. To be pleasing to God, one would have to obey all of God's laws perfectly. Who can do this? In his steadfast mercy, God sent his Son to obey perfectly all the laws in humanity's behalf. Not only that, he paid the penalty of death, even death on a cross. He did this even while we were yet sinners (Romans 5:8). Jesus died in our place, and as High Priest he sacrificed himself as a lamb of God on God's altar.

This does not mean that the cross changed God's mind from wrath to mercy. From the foundation of the world, God has loved his creation and sought in various ways to reconcile the world to himself. God loved us enough to pay for us the price of our sin, and the price was Calvary. Not knowing the extent of God's love and realizing that the justice of God was satisfied on the cross, we are persuaded and drawn by that love to return to him for forgiveness.

Forgiveness Made Personal

It is good to know that there is forgiveness with God. But how do we know we have been forgiven? How does it become a personal possession? Before a gift can be received, the person must want to receive the gift. God offers forgiveness as a gift, but are we receptive? God does not say, "Fulfill these conditions and then I will forgive you." No, he already for Jesus' sake has forgiven us and now offers it to us. To receive it we must be in a receptive condition. Here are steps to be taken before we will receive forgiveness:

1. **Consciousness of sin**. If we have no awareness of our sin, we will not desire forgiveness. Why should we? We have nothing for which to be forgiven. Because for some sin is a normal way of life, they do not acknowledge they are sinners. We see everybody sinning, so why shouldn't we? Or we say that it is human to err, and we are only being human. How can we get to see ourselves as sinners? One way is to look into the mirror of God's laws, the Decalogue. Then you will see that you have broken every one of the ten. Or look at the purity and perfection of Jesus, as Peter did

one time, and you will say with him, "Depart from me, Lord, for I am a sinful man" (Luke 5:8). Next, see the sin in other people and you will see your own. Nathan enabled David to see his sin against Uriah and Bathsheba by telling him a story of a poor man and his pet lamb. David could see the sin of the rich man, and then he saw his own sin by doing the same. Also, a vision of God's holiness will bring us to a realization of our sin. In Isaiah 6, he tells of his vision of the holiness of God and then he cries, "Woe is me, for I am a man of unclean lips."

2. **Contrition**. We may know that we have done wrong. So what? Who cares? Contrition means to be sorry, humiliated, and ashamed for those sins. Judas Iscariot was sorry he betrayed Jesus. He returned the thirty pieces of silver and admitted, "I have betrayed innocent blood." Being sorry for sins is not enough, but it is necessary for forgiveness. When two teenagers were arrested for theft, they were taken in a police car to the police station. A television camera showed them laughing and cutting up as though they had done nothing.

3. **Confession**. Are we sorry enough to confess our sins? We may know in our own minds and hearts that we are guilty but we will never admit it. Saint John shows us that confession is a prelude to forgiveness: "If we confess our sins, he will forgive ..." (1 John 1:9). If we do not confess, the sin begins to fester in us and may cause emotional and mental distress. The solution to guilt is forgiveness. The church provides us with an opportunity to confess either in public worship or in private pastoral counseling in a pastor's study. If we have nothing to confess, there is no need for forgiveness.

4. **Repentance**. It is not enough to confess you have sinned and are sorry for it. Following confession comes repentance. This calls for a change of mind as in *metanoia*, a Greek word meaning a change of mind. It calls for a radical turning from evil to good, from Satan to Christ. It means a radical internal revolution. It calls for a new heart and a new person. As John the Baptist preached, we must bring forth the fruit of repentance in terms of a changed life.

5. **Forgiveness**. According to Jesus, to be forgiven we must forgive others. In his prayer he taught us to say, "Forgive us ... as we forgive." He went further by saying that unless we forgive others, we cannot be forgiven by God. An unforgiving heart is a closed heart, and God cannot give forgiveness to a closed heart. Jesus taught us that if we have anything against a person and have a gift for God, we should leave the gift at the altar and go get right with the person in need of forgiveness. Then our gift will be acceptable.

6. **Restitution**. Christ expects us to undo, if possible, the harm we have done. When he came to Zacchaeus' home for dinner, Zacchaeus told Jesus that he would give half of his wealth to the poor and would restore fourfold what he had stolen. Likewise, we need to fix what we have broken, restore what we have stolen, and make amends for anything that hurt our neighbor.

In light of these conditions, we can see that forgiveness is a costly matter. To forgive truly is the hardest thing in the world to do. One time Jesus asked, "Which is easier to say, 'Your sins are forgiven' or 'Rise, take up your pallet and walk'?" It takes a miracle to forgive. That is why it is divine to forgive.

Doing Forgiveness

When in the Apostles' Creed we say that we believe in "the forgiveness of sins," we are saying that we believe that we ought to forgive those who sin against us just as God forgives us. If we are sincere in saying this, we need to practice it.

At the outset, we must admit that it is not easy to forgive some things that people do to us. For some the price of forgiving may be too much to pay. Corrie ten Boom was a prisoner in a Nazi concentration camp during the war years. She and others were degraded as human beings. Male guards would ogle women when they were compelled to take delousing showers. She made it through that hell. When the war was over and she was free again, she finally brought herself to where she could forgive her tormentors and to preach forgiveness. After a sermon in Munich, a man came to her with an outstretched hand and said, "Yes, it is wonderful that Jesus forgives us all our sins, just as you have preached." Then she remembered his face as one of the SS guards at the shower stalls.

Her hand froze at her side and she could not forgive him. She prayed, "Lord, forgive me. I cannot forgive." In answer to her prayer, her hand was unfrozen. The ice of hatred melted. She shook hands with him in token of her forgiveness. She forgave but it was not easy.

There are other experiences of forgiving others. Jacob sinned against his brother Esau; he stole Esau's birthright and his dying father's blessing. There was so much hatred as a result that Jacob had to flee to his uncle, Laban. The time came for Jacob to return. On the way, Jacob learned that Esau with 300 followers were on the way to him and he was scared of being killed. But Esau came with forgiveness so that Jacob said to Esau, "For truly to see your face is like seeing the face of God, with such favor have you received me" (Genesis 33:10). Likewise, Joseph brought his father and brothers to Egypt. When Jacob died, Joseph's brothers feared that Joseph would take revenge. But Joseph, with forgiveness, said to them, "You meant evil against me, but God meant it for good" (Genesis 50:17, 20).

How then can we bring ourselves to forgive? Consider these reasons:

1. **Obedience.** As Christians we are commanded to forgive: "As the Lord has forgiven you, so you also must forgive" (Colossians 3:13). Jesus gave us the example to follow when he prayed for his persecutors on the cross, "Father, forgive them ..." If we are faithful followers of Christ, we have no choice in the matter. Not to forgive is a sin of disobedience.

2. **Necessity.** Jesus made it clear that if we do not forgive, we cannot be forgiven. In the Sermon on the Mount Jesus said, "If you do not forgive men their trespasses, neither will your Father forgive your trespasses" (Matthew 6:15). Jesus is saying, forgive first and then I will forgive you. In other words, a forgiving person is forgiven.

3. **Expediency.** It does us more harm not to forgive than we can possibly do to our enemy. Hatred keeps us from forgiving. Hatred is an acid in the soul that corrodes our spirits and makes us miserable. For the sake of our own well-being, we need to cleanse our hearts of hatred and let love prevail. An unforgiving person is

never at peace with him/herself. The sin is relived time after time and each time the pain gets worse. If for no other reason, we should forgive for our own well-being.

4. **Love.** This is the ultimate and best reason to forgive. Jesus urged us to love our enemies. This love will not return evil for evil but good for evil. The best way to get rid of an enemy is to kill the person with kindness. When a pious old man was repeatedly told by his enemy that some day he would get even, the old man replied, "I'm going to kill him." His enemy laughingly replied, "He's a harmless old fool. I'm not afraid of him." In the following weeks the old man seized every opportunity to do good for his enemy. He prayed for him and sought opportunities to do him a good turn. One day the old man risked his life to save his enemy's child. "Well, you've done it! You have killed me, at least you killed the man I once was. Now let's be friends. What can I do for you?"

For all the good that forgiveness brings in our relationship with God and our fellow men, we emphatically say in the creed, I believe in "the forgiveness of sins."

The Forgiveness Of Sins

What does the Holy Spirit have to do with the forgiveness of sins? Doesn't God forgive sins? The Holy Spirit is God who forgives through the church. Jesus gave this authority when after the resurrection he said to the disciples, "Receive the Holy Spirit. If you forgive people's sins, they are forgiven" (John 20:22-23).

Forgiveness implies that we are sinners. What is a sin? There is disagreement as to what is or is not a sin. What do you think? Answer "Yes" or "No" to the following:

1. ___ Is it a sin if both parties consent?
2. ___ Is it a sin if a person feels good about it?
3. ___ Is it a sin if one thinks it is not wrong?
4. ___ Is it a sin if nobody knows about it?
5. ___ Is it a sin if society approves of it?
6. ___ Is it a sin if there is no law prohibiting it?
7. ___ Is it a sin if nobody is hurt by the sin?

Degrees Of Sin

Are some sins more serious than others? A poll shows that people vary in their estimate of a sin's seriousness:

	Major Sin %	Minor Sin %	Not A Sin %
1. Coveting a neighbor's spouse	83	8	2
2. Extramarital sex	83	11	3
3. Premarital sex	47	33	17
4. Lying	61	31	6
5. Swearing	23	57	19
6. Gambling	7	29	62
7. Sunday shopping	3	33	63

Who Can Forgive Sins?

Check your answer:
1. ___ Only God can forgive.
2. ___ Only an ordained pastor can pronounce forgiveness.
3. ___ A Spirit-filled lay person can forgive one's sins.
4. ___ The church can forgive sins.
5. ___ The Holy Spirit forgives through the Word and Sacraments as proclaimed by a pastor.

What Is Forgiveness?

Write "Yes" or "No."
1. ___ Forgiveness is pretending nothing has happened.
2. ___ Forgiveness is pretending that what was done to you did not hurt.
3. ___ Forgiveness is forgetting what happened.
4. ___ Forgiveness depends upon the offender's apology.
5. ___ Forgiveness is saying that the person was not to blame for the harm done.
6. ___ Forgiveness is a new relationship in which "there is nothing between us."
7. ___ Forgiveness is forgiving but never forgetting the sin.

Steps To Forgiveness

Which of these steps to forgiveness comes first, second, and so forth?
1. ___ Restitution
2. ___ Consciousness of sin
3. ___ Forgiving
4. ___ Contrition
5. ___ Repentance
6. ___ Confession

178

Chapter 13

The Word

The Means Of Grace

In the Apostles' Creed we confess that we believe in the forgiveness of sins. Through the forgiveness of sins we gain a right relationship with God. Forgiveness comes to us by what the church calls "the means of grace," consisting of Word and Sacraments. "Grace" is the infinite undeserved love of God for lost sinners. "Amazing Grace, how sweet the sound that saved a wretch like me." "Means" is a way grace (forgiveness) comes to us as channels or conduits bringing grace from God to the repentant sinner. If you visit Alaska, you will most likely see the oil pipeline that brings oil from north Alaska to the south at Valdez, where oil is put on tankers to be shipped south to a refinery. The pipeline is the means of bringing oil from the north to the south over hundreds of miles, just as Word and Sacraments bring grace to repentant believers.

The grace of God is as vast as an ocean. How can grace come to me, a small, finite believer? Whenever we want to pour a liquid from a large container to a small one, we use a funnel. The Word and Sacraments serve as a funnel bringing grace to the individual. Consider the diagram below.

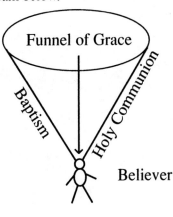

179

How can the forgiveness of God become a personal experience? How can a sinner be sure of God's forgiveness? How can one's guilt be removed and peace come to the heart through forgiveness? Consider the possibilities:

1. We can read about forgiveness in the Bible. Psalm 130:4 assures us that "There is forgiveness with you." It is good to know that God forgives, but how can one be sure he forgives me?

2. We can pray for forgiveness. David prayed, "Have mercy on me, O God ... blot out my transgressions" (Psalm 51:1). But how do I know my prayer was answered?

3. We can hear about forgiveness when the Word is preached and/or taught. A paralytic heard Jesus say, "Son, your sins are forgiven" (Mark 2:5). But I may never hear Jesus say that to me personally.

4. We can experience forgiveness through the Sacraments. It is the best way to know one is forgiven. Sacraments make forgiveness a specific, personal, and concrete assurance of pardon. It is something you can see, feel, and taste. Forgiveness comes in baptism: "Repent and be baptized ... so that your sins may be *forgiven*" (Acts 2:38). In Holy Communion forgiveness is received. Jesus said, "This is my blood of the covenant, which is poured out for many for the *forgiveness of sins*" (Matthew 26:28). The holy bread is the broken body and the cup is the shed blood of Christ. What more proof do we need that he died for the forgiveness of our sins?

The Word Of God

When we talk about the Word of God, what do we mean by "word"? What is the Word? The Word itself means communication, disclosure, and revelation. The Word is spoken and enacted. It is the way God reveals his nature and his will. He speaks only truth and his Word is grace. There is power in his Word, for it includes word and deed. God created the world by Word. " 'Let there be light' and it was so" (Genesis 1:14, 15). The word of the cross, according to Paul, is the power of salvation (1 Corinthians 1:18).

When we speak about "the Word of God," what do we mean? Just what is the Word of God? First, we mean that God's Word is

God's total revelation of himself from Genesis to Revelation. It includes God's mighty acts in the history of the Hebrews culminating in the founding of the church. The revelation goes from Adam and Eve to Abraham to Moses to David to Jesus.

Second, the Word of God is the incarnate Word, Jesus Christ. The Word is personalized in Jesus. "The Word became flesh and lived among us" (John 1:14). The grace, love, and truth of God were personified in Jesus. He is the final, ultimate, and perfect revelation of God the Father. Christ is the heart and center of the Bible. Luther explained that the Bible is the cradle that holds the Christ-child.

Third, the Word of God is the Bible, both Old and New Testaments. The Bible is the record of God's revelation through history. The Word is enclosed in the words of the Bible. The scriptures do not only contain the Word but are the Word, for container and contents cannot be separated any more than perfume can exist apart from the perfume bottle. In light of this, the Protestant Church holds that the Bible is the *sole* authority in matters of faith and life. The only textbook of the church is the Bible, which the church is mandated to preach and teach. Therefore, tradition, reason, and experience are secondary in authority. Reading, teaching, and preaching the Bible are essential. The tragedy of our day is biblical illiteracy as shown by the answers of certain students:

- "Noah's wife was the Joan of Ark."
- "Lot's wife was a pillar of salt by day and a ball of fire by night."
- "The sixth commandment: Thou shalt not admit adultery."
- "Epistles were the wives of the apostles."
- "A Christian has only one wife. This is called monotony."

Forms Of The Word

The Word of God comes to us in three forms: oral, visible, and written. The oral form comes in preaching, teaching, and witnessing. This is the original form before the Bible was written. The visible form comes in the Sacraments, Baptism and Eucharist. The written form comes last in the scriptures. The oral form comes to us through the ear. The visible form comes through the body by water, bread, and wine. The written form comes through the eye as we read it. The written form is the latest of the three. Each form is equally valid and authoritative. At a worship service all three forms may be received: preaching, teaching, reading the Lessons, and the reception of a Sacrament. The end result of the three forms is the creation and preservation of a Christian and the church. We may put the above in a diagram:

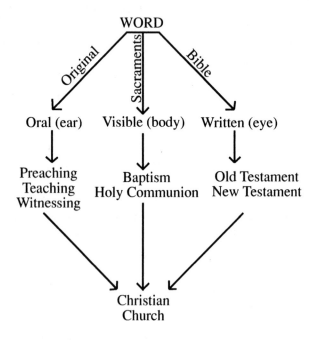

Interpreting The Word

When we read the Word (Bible), do we understand what we read? That was Philip's question to the Ethiopian eunuch while seated in his chariot: "Do you understand what you are reading?" (Acts 8:30). The Bible is not only to be read but to be properly interpreted. Faulty interpretation can lead to falsehood, dissension, and division among believers. The main problem is *eisegesis*, the reading of one's opinions into the text rather than getting the truth out of the text (*exegesis*). The average Bible reader needs to keep the following principles of interpretation in mind:

1. Interpret the Bible literally except when the Bible intends it to be taken figuratively. Example of figurative: Matthew 5:30 — "If your right hand causes you to sin, cut it off and throw it away." Example of literal: John 3:16 — "God so loved the world that he gave his only Son...."

2. Read the Bible in the light of the historical and cultural situation prevailing at the time of writing. For example: read Ruth in the light of the prejudice against Jews having foreign wives.

3. Read the Bible according to the type of literature you are reading. It may be poetry as the Psalms, history as in Samuel, a sermon as in Hebrews.

4. Read the Bible in the context of the whole Bible. It is wrong to take a verse or passage out of context. What does the rest of the Bible say about the subject you are reading? Check the parallel passages.

5. Read the Bible in the light of Christ. Not all things in the Bible are acceptable because they may not rise up to the teachings and spirit of Christ. He is the standard because he is the final and perfect revelation of God. The Old Testament promises the Messiah; the New Testament fulfills the promise in Jesus. Martin Luther said, "Remove Christ from the Scriptures and nothing is left."

Reading The Word Profitably

Why read the Bible if you get nothing out of it for your life and needs? To get the most out of Bible reading, consider the following suggestions:

1. Discipline yourself to a daily routine of Bible reading: same time, same place, apart from noise and interruptions.

2. Prepare for reading; be receptive by prayer before reading.

3. Relax in a comfortable chair and clear your mind of worldly concerns for the time being.

4. See the passage to be read in the context of the chapter or book.

5. Reflect and meditate on what you read. What is the Word in the words? A father once said to his son, "If you have only three minutes to read the Bible, spend one minute on reading and two minutes on reflection."

6. Apply the truth of the passage to your life. Ask the following questions of the passage:

- Any command for me to obey?
- Any promise for me to claim?
- Any sin for me to avoid?
- Any example for me to follow?
- Any prayer for me to echo?

The Word

What Are The Means?
1. Of getting water from the city reservoir to your house?

2. Of getting from Los Angeles to New York City?

3. Of getting an education?

4. Of getting the grace of God for your salvation?

Can You Find The Answers
See Matthew 17:1-8
1. Any command to obey?

2. Any promise to claim?

3. Any sin to avoid?

4. Any example to follow?

5. Any prayer to repeat?

What Is The Bible To You?
Check your answer(s):
1. ___ A human book designed to be read as literature.
2. ___ A paper pope that is errorless.
3. ___ A book of infallible truth.
4. ___ A cradle that holds Christ.
5. ___ The inspired Word of God.
6. ___ A Word of moral guidance.
7. ___ The final authority in matters of faith and life.
8. ___ The perfect and final revelation of God centered in Christ.

Where Would You Look —

1. To identify a person or event in the Bible?

2. To get the meaning of a word in the Bible?

3. To find a word or passage in the Bible?

4. To get the correct interpretation of a passage?

5. To get weights, dates, coins, and distances in the Bible?

6. To learn the customs and culture in the Bible?

To find the answers, go to your church library or Bible bookstore and examine a dictionary of the Bible, a word book, concordance, commentary, and a study Bible.

Chapter 14

Holy Baptism

Nature Of A Sacrament

On a visit to Washington, D.C., a family had a hard time finding a parking space. Finally they found an empty space in front of a small church. However, there was a sign reading: "No Parking. Violators will be baptized." When they read the small print at the bottom, "In the Potomac," they decided not to risk it. Apparently this church baptized by immersion and the Potomac was too much water for them!

In addition to the Word of God, Baptism, and the Lord's Supper, the church considers the Sacraments as a means of grace, the means of bringing the grace of God to repentant and believing sinners seeking salvation.

What is a sacrament? The word comes from the Latin *sacramentum*. When men entered the military, Roman soldiers took an oath of allegiance to Caesar as their only lord. Another word for sacrament is "covenant," "contract," or "testament." The Bible is divided into the Old Testament or old covenant and the New Testament or new covenant. It is the new covenant which Christ brought to us. When Jesus instituted the Lord's Supper, he said, "This cup is the *new covenant* in my blood." A sacrament is "a visible form of an invisible grace." It is essentially the Word of God with a visible sign, a visible form of the Word of God.

The Number Of Sacraments

Churches differ in the number of sacraments they celebrate. The Eastern Orthodox and Roman Catholic churches have seven, most Protestants have two, and some have none. The Baptist family of churches considers the sacraments as ordinances, not sacraments. Why do mainline Protestants have only two? They base their position on the Bible as the primary source of authority. The Bible has three conditions for a sacrament:

1. **Divine Command**. A sacrament is what Jesus commanded us to do. In baptism, Jesus commanded, "Go therefore and make disciples of all nations, baptizing them ..." (Matthew 28:19). Likewise, the command to observe the Lord's Supper: "Do this in remembrance of me" (1 Corinthians 11:24). Are marriage, confirmation, or ordination commanded by Christ?

2. **Divine Promise**. Jesus promised a blessing to those participating in a sacrament. For Baptism, he promised: "The one who believes and is baptized will be saved" (Mark 16:16). The promise given in the Holy Communion: "This is the blood of the covenant, which is poured out for many for the forgiveness of sins" (Matthew 26:28). Does Christ promise any blessing to a wedded couple?

3. **Earthly element**. Water is the sign for baptism; bread and wine are for the Lord's Supper. Is there any biblical sign connected with marriage, ordination, or penance? A ring is a sign of marriage, but it is not divinely ordered.

The Administration Of The Sacraments

In obedience to Christ's commands, the church administers the Sacraments through ordained ministers. For the sake of good order and the protection of the truth of the Sacraments, the administration is limited to the ordained ministers who at their ordination are authorized to preach the Word and to administer the Sacraments. The Augsburg Confession of 1530 A.D. states: "It is taught among us that nobody should publicly teach or preach or administer the sacraments of the church without a regular call" (Article XIV). An exception is made in the administration of Baptism when a person is dying and a pastor is not available. A Christian layman has the authority to baptize in such a case, and the baptism is to be reported to a church.

The Bible And Baptism

What is the meaning of the Sacrament of Holy Baptism? The Bible explains:

1. **Baptism is an adoption** — Galatians 4:5

Because of his love, God adopts a sinner as his child. By Baptism we become members of God's family. Now the baptized can

188

cry, "Abba, Father." Now we can pray "Our Father." If we are the adopted children of God, then we will always be his. Therefore there is no need of a second baptism as the Nicene Creed confesses: "We acknowledge *one* baptism for the forgiveness of sins." No matter what we do or how wicked we may become, God remains our Father. We may fall from faith but can never fall from grace, because God is forever faithful to us. Years ago, a popular television show was *All In The Family*. Archie Bunker wants his grandson to be baptized. Michael, the father, objects to Archie's conniving to get the child baptized. Archie argues, "What's the matter, you were baptized, weren't you?" "Yes," Michael replies, "but I renounce my baptism." "You can't do that," says Archie. "You can renounce your belly button, but it won't go away." Baptism is permanent and indelible because God is faithful and will never disown his child.

2. Baptism is a death and resurrection — Romans 6:3-4

Baptism is death to the old, sinful self. It is symbolized by immersion. The sinner is held under the water symbolically until he/she dies and is raised as a new creature in Christ. A prison chaplain baptized a repentant man for molesting his ten-year-old daughter. The only baptismal font in the prison was a plastic-lined coffin. The chaplain lowered him into the coffin of death and raised him to new life in Christ. After the baptism the prisoner said, "I'm now a free man."

3. Baptism is a new birth — John 3:7

Jesus told Nicodemus that he must be born anew to enter the Kingdom of God. This happens when a person is baptized. As the Holy Spirit came to Jesus at his baptism in the form of a dove, so the Holy Spirit is given to the baptized. Baptism is one of the mighty acts of God in giving new life to the person baptized. A baptism is not to be received or witnessed with shut eyes and bowed heads as though it were a prayer time. Our heads and eyes should look up and see the Holy Spirit coming like a dove descending on the person. At baptism a person becomes a new individual, a Christian, a child of God. Hallelujah!

4. Baptism is an initiation — 1 Corinthians 12:13

When we are baptized, we are incorporated into the body of Christ, the church. Automatically we become members of a church. A Christian and the church are inseparable. One cannot be a Christian outside the church, for the church is the society of the saved. This applies also to children who are baptized. They are not probation members but real members of the church. Baptism is the initiation into Christ and the church.

5. Baptism is a covenant — Jeremiah 32:38

Baptism is a covenant or contract made between God and the believer. It is a bonding of Christ with the repentant one, just as a mother and a newborn baby have a time of bonding. Baptism establishes a relationship with God by faith in Christ. God is our God and we are his people. We belong to him and he belongs to us.

To understand Baptism as a covenant it is necessary to see this covenant in the perspective of past covenants God made with his people.

(1) The old covenant made between God and the nation of Israel:

Name	Promise	Sign
Noah (Genesis 9:8-13)	No future flood of world	Rainbow
Abraham (Genesis 17:9-10)	A great nation	Circumcision
Moses (Exodus 19:3-6, 24:12)	Promised Land	Stone tablets
Jeremiah (31:31-34)	New covenant	Heart

(2) The new covenant made between God and the believer:

Jesus	Fulfillment	Empty tomb
Baptism (original)	Salvation	Water
Holy Communion (renewed)	Forgiveness	Bread, wine

(3) Promises of the new covenant:

God's Promises (Benefits)		Believer's Promises (Responsibilities)	
Forgiveness		Repentance ↑	
Eternal life	↓	Faith	
Deliverance	Grace		Faith

Infant Baptism

If repentance and faith are necessary conditions for baptism, why baptize infants? I was twelve days old when I was baptized. What did I know about repentance and faith? The church has reasons for baptizing babies:

1. The tradition of the church since apostolic times. In the New Testament there are accounts of families with children being baptized.

2. The universal practice of the church. The vast majority of churches baptize infants: Roman Catholic, Eastern Orthodox, most Protestant churches.

3. Children need forgiveness of original sin.

4. Children as well as adults need to become children of God by spiritual rebirth through the Holy Spirit received at Baptism.

5. Children need to become members both of God's Kingdom and the church.

Adult Responsibilities In Infant Baptism

Since it is necessary for children to have repentance and faith to be baptized, the church calls upon adult Christians to be sponsors of the children. The sponsors (parents, godparents, members of the church) make the promises of repentance and faith in the child's behalf. The sponsors assume the responsibilities to see that the child is raised in the Christian faith, taught the Ten Commandments, taught how to pray, what to believe, and brought to the church for worship and religious instruction in the church school.

These responsibilities continue until the child is confirmed at an age when the child can understand the faith and assume responsibilities for him/herself. At confirmation the youth now confesses faith in Christ and vows loyalty to the church and her teachings. For the youth it is as great a day as when a person is baptized.

Infant baptism is not a private affair. It is an act of the church and it is to be administered when the church is assembled. Church members also are sponsors of the child in baptism. The church has the responsibility to nurture the child's faith through worship, teaching, and fellowship in the church.

The Seal Of Baptism
The External Seal: Water

In the world, an agreement or contract (covenant) must be signed by both parties. To make it legal a seal is placed on the document by a notary public. The baptismal covenant is sealed when the water is applied to the candidate.

Among the denominations there is a disagreement as to the amount of water and the method of applying the water. One church requires a body of water so that the person can be immersed. Unless the person is immersed, there is no baptism. A Baptist and Lutheran boy were playing church. They sang hymns, preached, and took up an offering. Then they wanted a baptism. One lad suggested baptizing some kittens nearby. The Baptist boy filled up a tub with water and immersed two of the kittens. A third gave him opposition. The cat scratched, bit, and drew some blood. Finally the Baptist lad said to the Lutheran: "Here, you baptize this one and let it go to hell." Immersion is based on the word "baptize," which usually means to immerse, but it also means to wash, as in Luke 11:38: "The Pharisee was amazed to see that he did not first wash (*baptizo*) before dinner."

Most churches agree that the kind or the amount of water does not save a person but it is the Word that does it. Some churches accept any of the three modes of applying the water: immersion, pouring, and sprinkling.

The Internal Seal: Holy Spirit

As in Jesus' baptism, when we are baptized we receive the Holy Spirit. The Spirit is the seal of our salvation received in baptism. Paul wrote, "In him you also ... were marked with the seal of the promised Holy Spirit" (Ephesians 1:13). The Spirit is the guarantee of God's acceptance (2 Corinthians 1:22). The seal of the Holy Spirit is referred to as "earnest," a first installment, or as in a real estate deal, it is the down payment that secures the purchase of the property. When we receive the Holy Spirit at baptism, we can be sure of our acceptance by God.

The Benefits Of Baptism

1. Baptism gives assurance of being a child of God through his adoption. It answers the basic questions of life: "Who am I?" and "Where am I headed?"

2. Baptism means salvation. "He who believes and is baptized shall be saved." Baptism is a cleansing from sin, and guilt is

192

removed. The church teaches that baptism is necessary for salvation, for without grace we cannot be saved. Baptism is a means of grace.

3. Baptism is a channel for the Holy Spirit. At baptism the Holy Spirit comes to us and creates a new person, a new creature in Christ. We are born again.

4. Baptism promises eternal life. A baptized person faithful to death can be certain that heaven is the ultimate destiny.

To those baptized, the church says, "Remember your baptism." To those not baptized, "Repent and believe." Like Jesus and Paul, seek to be baptized and receive the grace that saves.

Holy Baptism

Questions To Stretch Your Mind

Think seriously on these questions and, if possible, discuss them with a group. Read the chapter again for answers.

1. Should adults only be baptized? If not, why not?

2. What is the proper way to apply the water in baptism?

3. Is baptism an ordinance or a sacrament? What is the difference?

4. Is infant baptism a dedication of the child to God or the incorporation into the church? What do you mean by "incorporation"?

5. Is one saved before baptism or during it?

6. Can baptism be administered by a lay Christian?

7. May baptism be repeated? What does the Nicene Creed say?

8. What is the difference between water baptism and spirit baptism? Can it be both?

9. Is baptism optional for salvation?

10. What happens to a child who dies before baptism?

11. Is it possible for a dead person to be baptized?

12. Since Jesus was without sin, why did he ask John the Baptist to baptize him?

The Bible And Baptism

Look up the following passages dealing with baptism to learn its teachings.

1. Galatians 4:5 — Is baptism an expression of God's love for the lost sinner?

2. Romans 6:3-4 — How can a person die and later be raised to new life?

3. John 3:7 — How is a person born again? How does it feel to be born again?

4. 1 Corinthians 12:13 — Baptism makes a person a member of the church which is the body of Christ. Is it possible to be a Christian apart from the church?

5. Jeremiah 32:38 — In baptism God becomes your God and you become God's child. How and when is this relationship established?

Chapter 15

Holy Communion

Before going to the electric chair a criminal indicates what he would like for his last meal. Some murderers choose steak, hamburgers, shrimp, half a bottle of red wine, or chicken. In 1431 Joan of Arc, burned at the stake in France, chose the Holy Communion for her last dinner. A devout Christian wants to close out life on earth by having Holy Communion administered in one's dying day. Why? Because Holy Communion is a means of grace which brings God's mercy in terms of forgiveness and eternal life. Above all, Holy Communion provides a mystical union with Christ. The Holy Communion is the holiest of the holy, the epitome of religious experience, the narthex of heaven.

On the other hand, in the history of the church the Holy Communion has been a divisive and controversial subject. For giving the cup to worshipers, John Huss was burned by the church at a stake on the shore of Lake Constance. Luther and Zwingli parted company after disagreeing about the real presence of Christ in the sacrament. Today churches are divided by questions concerning Communion to infants, the frequency of Communion, the use of lay administration, the real presence of Christ in the elements of bread and wine, and the downgrading of the sermon in favor of a weekly celebration of the Lord's Supper.

The Relation Of Baptism To Holy Communion

Baptism and Holy Communion are both Sacraments and means of grace along with the Word of God. Baptism is the original covenant made between God and a believer. Holy Communion is a renewal of the baptismal covenant. Though we at our baptism promised God repentance and faith, we by our sins have not kept the promise. Therefore, the covenant was broken on the believer's part. Though forgiven when baptized, we continue to sin after baptism.

Jesus provided the Holy Communion for sins committed after baptism or since the last communion.

Baptism is the sacrament of initiation; Holy Communion is the sacrament of continuation. Baptism is to faith as birth is to physical life; Holy Communion is to faith as food is for physical life. Baptism makes us members of the Kingdom of God; Holy Communion keeps us in the Kingdom. Baptism is a once-in-a-lifetime experience, for adoption occurs only once; Holy Communion is repeatedly received as a guilty heart feels the need of forgiveness.

The Passover And The Holy Communion

The Holy Communion is an outgrowth of the Old Testament Passover (Exodus 12). Before the departure from Egypt, Moses directed that each family should kill a one-year-old male lamb without blemish. A lamb was slaughtered and some of the blood was put on the doorposts and lintel of Jewish homes. "It is the passover of the Lord" (Exodus 12:11). An angel of death was to strike down every firstborn child in Egypt. "When I see the blood, I will pass over you" (12:13). For seven days the Jews were to eat unleavened bread. To this day it is the major annual feast of Jews. It observes the liberation from slavery.

To prepare for the annual Passover meal, Jesus sent Peter and John to prepare the meal in a secret upper room in Jerusalem. During the meal Jesus instituted the Lord's Supper by saying the bread is his body and the wine his blood.

In Saint Paul's time the Holy Communion was celebrated in combination with a meal called "Agape" or "Love Feast." Before the meal the bread of Communion was served. The meal followed and then the cup was administered. Abuses crept in during the meal. Some did not have enough to eat and others became drunk. To solve the problem Paul told the people to eat at home before coming to the Lord's Supper. "If you are hungry, eat at home" (1 Corinthians 11:34).

As the Passover signified the deliverance from bondage in Egypt, the Lord's Supper means our deliverance from the slavery of sin. As the blood of the lamb caused the angel of death to fly over the Hebrew homes, Jesus is the Lamb of God whose blood was shed to deliver us from death resulting from our sins.

Names Of The Sacrament

The Holy Communion is known by several names. Each name gives an understanding of the sacrament.

1. Lord's Supper

The Lord's Supper was the last supper Jesus had with his twelve. It was really more than a supper. It was more like a banquet. Jesus was the host and the food consisted of his body and blood. It was a wonderful feast like none other. This is still today's understanding of this sacrament. The pastor, representing Christ, is the host. He is authorized by the church to serve the food. When the people gather at the Communion rail, it is known as a "table." In recent years the entire congregation is considered one table and the administration is continuous. The Lord's Supper is the time and place to feed the soul with the Bread of Life.

2. Sacrament Of The Altar

The Lord's Supper is also known as the Sacrament of the Altar. This tells us that the Holy Communion is a sacrament, a means of grace. A sacrament is a covenant between God and a believer. The covenant made at baptism was broken by our sin and we need to have it renewed, which is done in the Holy Communion. In receiving the Holy Communion a penitent is restored in his/her relationship with God.

It is called "Altar" because the altar is the symbol of sacrifice. We bring our sacrifice of praise and thanks to the altar. The benefits of Christ's sacrifice on the cross come to us in this sacrament. The physical elements of bread and wine are placed on the altar and the people come to the altar to receive them. Christ serves both as priest and victim that is sacrificed for the sin of the world.

3. Holy Communion

The Sacrament of the Altar is called "holy" because we commune with the holy Jesus. It is also called "Communion," meaning "fellowship" or being one with Christ. It is a mystical union with him as Christ said, "Abide in me as I abide in you" (John 15:4).

If we are to have communion with Christ, he needs to be present in the bread and wine. Denominations differ on the question of the real presence of Christ in the sacrament. First, there is the literal presence of Christ called "transubstantiation." The physical substance of the elements turn miraculously into the body and blood of Christ during the Words of Institution.

A second view is the absence of the presence of Christ. The bread and wine are only symbols of his presence. Then the Holy Communion is a memorial celebration and an act of commitment rather than a means of grace. When Jesus said, "This is my body," it is held that "is" means "signifies." With this view, Holy Communion is an open Communion to all who want to remember Jesus. When Mary McCarthy told Flannery O'Connor that the Holy Communion was only symbolic and could therefore be accepted, O'Connor replied, "Well, if it's a symbol, to hell with it!"

A third view says there is a spiritual presence in the bread and wine. They are the true body and blood of Christ while the physical characteristics remain. In, with, and under the bread and wine is the real presence. It is like an electric iron which one uses. It has a chrome base and a black handle with an electric cord. Before plugging it in, the iron is cold. After plugging it in for a few minutes, it has a new element — heat! In the same way, the bread and wine are the same, but the presence of Christ comes into the elements. The faith of the communicant acknowledges the presence of Christ in the bread and wine.

4. Eucharist

Since the second Vatican Council held in the 1960s, the name "Eucharist" has become popular among some Protestant denominations. "Eucharist" comes from a Greek word meaning "thanksgiving." When we remember the life, cross, and resurrection of Jesus we have every reason to be thankful to God. As related to the Lord's Supper, the name is theologically inadequate. "Eucharist" is a sacrificial term indicating thanks, praise, joy, and celebration. It is the human response to God. But the true meaning of Holy Communion is sacramental. The Supper's significance is not in what we say or do but it is what God says and does in Christ. It is not a matter of earth to heaven but heaven to earth. It is Christ who comes to us in bread and wine for our forgiveness and eternal life.

This current term "Eucharist" has for many churches changed the meaning of the Lord's Supper. A change has been made in the chancel. The altar traditionally was placed at the east wall of the church. Now the altar is freestanding and moved to the entrance of the chancel. The altar has been turned into a table to hold the Communion vessels and elements. It is no longer so much a sacrament as a celebration. It is celebrated with joy, praise, and thanksgiving. Repentance is no longer required. There is no need for a confession of sins because there are no sins to confess. If there are no sins to confess, there is no need for forgiveness. This concept of "Eucharist" has led to infant Communion. The leaders of the Protestant Church are insisting upon celebrating Eucharist at each worship service, wedding, funeral, and gathering. Since the traditional service is an hour long, the Eucharist demands a "hurry up" service by cutting the liturgy, shortening the sermon, the use of intinction, lay administrators, abandonment of kneeling at the altar rail, and establishing "stations" in various parts of the church rather than coming to the altar. This is resulting in a mechanical, routine affair with little or no time for meditation and reflection at the altar rail. The Holy Communion has become a routine ritual, doing it as fast as possible in an *ex opere operatum* manner.

The Five R's Of Holy Communion

To help us remember the meaning of Holy Communion, we can think of the meaning of this sacrament in five words beginning with "R."

1. **Remembrance**. Twice Jesus said when instituting the Supper, "Do this in remembrance of me." This makes the Communion into a memorial dinner. When we remember (relive) the life, death, and resurrection of Jesus, we are filled with gratitude and joy.

2. **Renewal**. The Lord's Supper is a sacrament which binds God and the believer into a personal relationship. Since our sins break the baptismal covenant, we need to renew it. The Lord's Supper is the remaking of the covenant because of our repentance, confession, and reception of the Sacrament.

3. **Repentance.** The Holy Communion is only for sinners who are sorry for their sins, confess them, and in repentance turn away from them to a more Christlike style of life. Some churches no longer require repentance for admission to the Lord's Table. One church's Sunday bulletin said, "We welcome all baptized Christians who have faith in the real presence of our Lord in the sacrament to come." Just so you are baptized — no need of repentance! The announcement should have read "repentant believers."

4. **Remission.** When Jesus passed the cup at the Last Supper, he said, "This is my blood of the new testament, which is shed for many for the remission of sins" (Matthew 26:28, KJV). His shed blood and broken body are the proof of his love in forgiving our sins. At the close of the Communion service, repentant sinners leave free of guilt and at peace with God.

5. **Reunion.** The height of the religious experience in Holy Communion is the reunion with Christ. We have a glorious mystical union with him. We feel and know he is really present in the bread and wine. When we leave the church, we can say, "We have been with Jesus."

The Administration Of Holy Communion

Who is eligible to give the bread (body) and wine (blood) to those who come to receive the Holy Communion? Protestants believing in the biblical priesthood of believers would answer any faithful Christian. However, the church has given this privilege to the ordained clergy to prevent abuses and to control the administration. In the Augsburg Confession of 1530 the privilege was given to the ordained: "It is taught among us that nobody should teach or preach or administer the sacraments in the church without a regular call." The action was not based on the belief that ministers are more holy than lay people. It is done for the sake of good order. The church authorizes clergy at their ordination to preach the Word and administer the Sacraments.

Ordained ministers are expected to lead holy lives and lay people look to the ordained as moral examples to be imitated. If the person administering the body and blood of Christ is not worthy of imitation, damage is done to the faith of the communicant.

One of my daughters wrote me some time ago about her trouble communing in her church. A layman administering Communion was having an affair with a married woman in the choir. He is also the chairman of the Administrative Board. His wife gives the children's sermons. This layman had so disturbed her spirit that she considered leaving the church.

What Is Administered?

1. **Bread**. Jesus distributed bread to the twelve in the Upper Room on the night he was betrayed. He said, "This is my body broken for you." It was unleavened bread in keeping with the Passover meal. Today unleavened bread is appropriate. Leaven puffs up bread. Unleavened bread is flat. It symbolizes humility rather than the leavened bread of pride. Again, Jesus said, "Take heed and beware of the leaven of the Pharisees and Sadducees" (Matthew 16:6). The leaven represented the wickedness of the religious leaders. The unleavened bread of Communion is the sinless bread of Christ. It is administered to the mouth or the hand. Receiving the bread in the mouth means the person feels unworthy to touch the body of Christ or it symbolizes that the person is a babe in Christ and like a baby, the child of God needs to be fed to the mouth.

2. **Wine**. Jesus passed a cup of wine to the disciples, saying, "This cup is the new covenant in my blood." Jesus used wine as freely as we drink water. He turned water into wine for a wedding at Cana. While on the cross, he was given wine. Until modern times the church universally used wine for Communion because Jesus did. In the years of temperance and prohibition of the late nineteenth and early twentieth centuries, grape juice was substituted for wine. A Methodist, Thomas Welch of Vineland, New Jersey, offered to donate to the churches unfermented grape juice. Methodist, Baptist, and Presbyterian churches began to use grape juice in order to have a nonalcoholic Communion.

The wine is administered by a common cup to symbolize the oneness of Christians in Christ. Jesus passed one cup to the twelve. Because of fear of passing germs, some churches began using small individual cups. To retain the symbolism of the common cup and yet to avoid passing germs, a common cup with a pouring lip was designed. In this case, the pastor filled each cup at the altar rail. A third method is intinction. To shorten the time of administration, the bread was dipped in wine and then administered to the mouth of the communicant.

To receive these elements, it is traditional for the people to kneel at the altar rail. Kneeling indicates humility and unworthiness in the presence of the risen Lord.

Upon receiving bread and wine, the communicant usually responds with an audible "amen" indicating that the person accepts the bread and wine as the body and blood of Christ for the forgiveness of sins and union with Christ.

Worthiness To Receive Communion

While I was a young pastor, some of my people neglected to come to Communion because they considered themselves unworthy. My answer to them was, "The Holy Communion is for repentant sinners only." Saint Paul faced the problem of worthiness in the Corinthian church. He wrote, "Whoever, therefore, eats the bread and drinks the cup of the Lord in an unworthy manner ..." (1 Corinthians 11:27). It is a question also in today's church.

1. Are little children worthy of receiving Communion? Some churches think so. At the 1997 assembly of the Evanglical Lutheran Church in America, this church took action permitting congregations to administer Communion to children as soon as they are baptized. Can a little child understand the meaning of Communion, or the meaning of repentance and faith? Can a child examine him/herself to see if sin has been committed, as Saint Paul writes: "Examine yourselves and only then eat the bread and drink the cup" (1 Corinthians 11:28)? It can mean nothing spiritually to a child as in the case of little Ellen. She was taken for the first time to church. It happened to be Communion Sunday. Her mother took Ellen with her to the altar and took the elements. When they walked back to their pew, she leaned over to a boy behind her and whispered, "I had a coke!" If a child is worthy of taking Communion the child need not have a "first Communion," catechetical instruction, or confirmation.

2. Are older children worthy of Communion before they are confirmed? Let's assume the child was baptized when an infant. When the child reaches the appropriate age and has received instruction in the catechism, he/she is confirmed. At confirmation the youth accepts the responsibilities of baptism taken for him/her by the sponsors. At confirmation the youth confesses his/her faith and accepts Christ as Savior and Lord. The youth has now fulfilled the human side of the baptismal covenant. Since the Holy Communion is a renewal of the covenant, how can one renew a covenant that was never made?

3. Is a person worthy of Communion only on the basis of having been baptized? In the Sunday church bulletin, a church invites people to the altar on the basis of their baptism. When Jesus instituted the Lord's Supper, he said, "This cup is the new covenant in my blood, shed for you and for all people for the forgiveness of sin." If forgiveness is to be received, there must be confession of sins, contrition for those sins, and repentance for committing the sins. A baptized person can be one who says, "I sin — so what?"

4. The consequences of communing unworthily are disastrous. Paul writes, "For all who eat and drink without discerning the body, eat and drink judgment against themselves" (1 Corinthians 11:29). The big question is, what is the "body"? Some say it is the church as the body of Christ. Others claim the "body" is Christ. We are eating and drinking the body of Christ, not the church. That is why unworthy partaking of Communion is a "judgment" on us, as Paul described it as making them "weak and ill and some have died." To be worthy of taking Communion, we must come as penitent sinners to be assured of the remission of our sins.

Frequency Of Communion

How often should we receive the Holy Communion? When instituting the sacrament, Jesus said, "Do this, as *often* as you drink it." Paul adds, "For as *often* as you eat this bread and drink the cup ..." (1 Corinthians 11:25, 26). "Often" does not tell us the number of times we should commune. In a 1996 study of the rate of Communion in the Evangelical Lutheran Church in America, it was learned that 21 percent offered it weekly, 15 percent monthly, and 3 percent quarterly.

205

Today the trend is to offer Communion weekly as a part of the regular worship service. The leadership of some denominations are pushing to have Holy Communion available at all worship services, weddings, funerals, and church assemblies. It is maintained that the sacrament was offered weekly in the early church. Dr. John Reumann, a highly respected New Testament scholar, says in his book *The Supper of the Lord*, published by Fortress in 1985:

> *A celebration every Sunday or even daily of what is to be "the central act of worship" for the primitive church is widely asserted. The fact of the matter is that we have little evidence and do not know how often or when Communion was held in the New Testament period, or when, let alone how frequently, believers received the Lord's Supper. The assumption is too easy, however, and to be resisted that every Sunday was a Eucharist, or that every worship service was sacramental.* (pp. 47, 48)

What is the answer to the frequency of Communion? It is reasonable and necessary to hold that each Sunday the sacrament should be available but not necessarily at the regular worship service when some feel they are expected to partake and are embarrassed to leave when the Communion liturgy begins. Some churches schedule a Communion service every Sunday at an early service, or between services, or after a service.

Is the answer: Come to Communion when you feel the need of it, when you have a need to relieve your guilt, when you have a strong desire to be united with Christ? Taking Communion should never be a routine or ritual matter as just going through the motions and meaning nothing to you. To be meaningful calls for preparation: an examination of oneself, a hunger and thirst for restoring oneself with God through the assurance of forgiveness and union with Christ. This was Martin Luther's position on the frequency of taking Communion. In a sermon of March 14, 1522, he said, "So we do not always find that we are fit [to receive Communion]; today I have the grace and am fit for it, but not tomorrow. Indeed, it may be that for *six months* I may have no desire or fitness for it [Holy Communion]" (quoted in Lull, *Luther's Basic Theological Writings*, p. 438).

Holy Communion

Holy Communion Disagreements

Are there any disagreements in your congregation related to Holy Communion? Check your answer(s).

1. ___ Infant Communion
2. ___ Every Sunday Communion
3. ___ Lay administratio
4. ___ Longer than one-hour service
5. ___ Understanding of the Real Presence
6. ___ Meditation instead of sermon

Name Of The Sacrament

Which name of the Sacrament do you prefer? Defend your choice. Check your answer.

1. ___ Lord's Supper
2. ___ Holy Communion
3. ___ Sacrament of the Altar
4. ___ Eucharist

The Five R's Of Communion

The Sacrament can be explained in five words beginning with "R." Can you list the five and explain each one?

1. R_____

2. R_____

3. R_____

4. R_____

5. R_____

The Supper's Administration
Check your choice:

The person who administers the elements:
1. ___ Self-service
2. ___ Lay person
3. ___ Ordained clergy

The bread — which do you prefer and why?
1. ___ Loaf of bread
2. ___ Wafer of leavened bread
3. ___ Wafer of unleavened bread

The wine — which do you prefer?
1. ___ Grape juice
2. ___ Wine
3. ___ Common cup
4. ___ Individual cup
5. ___ Intinction

Worthiness To Partake
If you were the pastor, would you invite the following to the Lord's Table?
1. ___ Sinners
2. ___ Repentant baptized sinners
3. ___ Baptized only
4. ___ Infants
5. ___ Unconfirmed youth
6. ___ Nonmembers of your church

Frequency Of Reception
How often would you like to receive the Holy Communion? Check your answer.
1. ___ Weekly
2. ___ Monthly
3. ___ Quarterly
4. ___ Annually
5. ___ Your need for forgiveness and oneness with Christ

Chapter 16

The Resurrection Of The Body

According to a traditional teaching in the Bible, Christ will return unexpectedly to earth, and all the dead will rise from their graves to be judged along with those living on earth at the time of his coming. The wicked will go to hell and the faithful will go to heaven. Christ's people will share in his victory over sin and death and will go with him to a new heaven (Revelation 21:1). In keeping with this teaching, the Apostles' Creed has us say we believe in "the resurrection of the body."

However, the Bible never speaks of the resurrection of the body, but rather of the resurrection "of the dead" or "from the dead." The Apostles' Creed puts emphasis on the "body," which makes this doctrine the most difficult in this creed. It seems to imply a physical resurrection of the dead. This causes modern people some concern and perplexity. How can billions of dead people come to life instantly at Jesus' return? How can the dead bones take on skin, muscles, and nerves? What of those, like unknown soldiers whose bodies have been blown to smithereens and scattered in unknown and distant places? How can bodies come back to normal existence that have been eaten by animals or cannibals? What of those bodies buried at sea? When bodies are cremated and scattered to the winds, how can they become flesh and blood persons again?

Why was the "resurrection of the body" put into the Apostles' Creed? A creed has usually been prepared to oppose heresy and to defend the biblical truth. The authors of the creed placed this phrase in the creed to oppose the prevalent Greek and Gnostic views of the body held at that time. The Greeks and Gnostics held that the physical body was evil because all matter was evil. The body was considered the prison of the soul. At the death of the body, the soul was released for an immortal existence. The human body was despised and considered inferior to the soul. Gnosticism, a popular heresy during New Testament times, longed to free the pure soul from a dead body. The Greek mind held to the immortality of the soul apart from the body, whereas the Christian view deals with the resurrection of the body.

The Resurrection

At the beginning of the church, some did not believe in the resurrection of the dead or from the dead. Paul refers to this segment of the church: "Now if Christ is preached as raised from the dead, how can some of you say that there is no resurrection of the dead?" (1 Corinthians 15:12).

Some hold that the resurrection of the dead has already taken place. They believed that the resurrection took place at baptism. At this time a person dies to self and is resurrected with Christ into a new life. The people who held that the resurrection of the dead has already taken place were convinced that they would never die.

Again, those who denied the resurrection of the dead held to the belief that our lives would continue in our children. Parents will live in their children and grandchildren for ages to come. Eternal existence, then, is in the continuation of the human race. If we do not die because we live in our children, there is no need for a resurrection from the dead.

On the other hand, the Apostles' Creed expresses the orthodox faith that there is a resurrection of the dead. Christians do believe in a resurrection, even as Jesus was raised from the dead. Why do Christians believe it?

1. If there is no resurrection from the dead, we have no hope or assurance that there is life after death. Then we will die and forever remain dead. Death and not Christ will be the victor, and we will not in triumph ask, "O death, where is your sting? O grave, where is your victory?"

2. Christians believe in the resurrection of the dead because our resurrection confirms the resurrection of Jesus. Paul put it this way: "If there is no resurrection of the dead, then Christ has not been raised" (1 Corinthians 15:13). Because Christ has been raised, we, too, shall be raised from the dead. He is the first fruits of the dead, our pioneer in overcoming death. Everything hinges on his

resurrection. Saint Paul says if Christ was not raised, we are still in our sins. Without the resurrection of Christ we have no Gospel, no Savior, and no hope of eternal life. Because Christ has risen, we as people in Christ will rise also.

3. It is necessary for the non-Christian dead to be raised for the final judgment. The Bible teaches that Christ will return to wind up history. Without a resurrection people would escape the consequences of their sins. Death could be a cop-out from justice. They could get away with murder and suffer no results. Take, for instance, the case of two men who broke into a home and killed husband and wife. They escaped in a stolen car. When police surrounded them, they committed suicide. Death was their escape from human justice. If there were no resurrection of the dead, they would also escape divine justice.

When or what causes this resurrection of the dead? Do the dead raise themselves? Who has the power to bring life out of death? For the answer we need to go back to the beginning of this third article of the creed: "I believe in the Holy Spirit." The Spirit created the "holy catholic church." Through the church's means of grace, Word and sacraments, the Holy Spirit provides the "forgiveness of sins, the resurrection of the body, and the life everlasting."

No one but God can cause resurrection. It was God who raised Jesus (Acts 2:24). Today God raises us from the dead through his Spirit. God the Spirit is life and life-giving. Note what Paul says: "If the Spirit of him who raised Jesus from the dead dwells in you, he who raised Christ Jesus from the dead will give life to your mortal bodies also through his Spirit which dwells in you" (Romans 8:11).

When does this resurrection take place? The final resurrection is associated with the Parousia, the second coming of Christ. In 1 Thessalonians 4, Paul says that at the end of time Christ will descend from heaven accompanied by an archangel's call and the trumpet of God. The nations will gather before him for judgment.

There is also a resurrection from the dead for those who die in Christ now. In 1 Thessalonians 4, Paul says that when Christ comes again, he "will bring with him those who have fallen asleep" (the dead). In other words, those who die in Christ before the Parousia will rise and be with Christ in heaven. This is in keeping with Jesus' promise to the repentant thief on the cross, "Today you shall be with me in paradise." In his letters Paul says that to be in the body on earth is to be absent from the Lord, and that it is gain to die because it means fellowship with Christ in heaven. This means that a Christian does not remain in a grave until Christ's return. At the time of death, a Christian is resurrected from death to be with Christ. When the end of the world comes, a Christian will return with Christ for the final wrap-up of history.

The Physical Body

According to scripture a human is a unity of body, mind, and soul. They are interrelated and interdependent. Each part affects the other. The condition of the body affects the mind, and the soul affects both body and mind. They should not be separated as entities in themselves. The whole person is a union of these three elements. Modern medical science supports this fact, for treatment in the restoration of health calls for all three to be considered. It is known as psychosomatic medicine. To exist a soul must have a body. It may be illustrated in the diagram:

Because Christians are citizens of two worlds, we have two bodies. To live on earth in this physical world, we were given a physical body. According to this body, a Christian is limited to a physical body. In the New Testament the Greek word used for the physical body is *sarx*. It is usually translated as "flesh." Paul uses *sarx* as the seat of sinful desires. According to Genesis, the physical body was made out of dust and it is scheduled to return to dust. Along with all of nature, death is programmed in it.

The other body is the resurrected spiritual body. The Greek word for this body is *soma*. It refers to the total person, which includes body and soul. As we were given a physical body to live in a physical world, we are given a spiritual body to live in the future spiritual world of love, truth, and God. When astronauts walked on the moon, they were in a world different from the earth. On the moon there was no oxygen. In order to live the astronauts had to carry their own life support system of oxygen. Humans were not made to live on other planets. In the same way, earthly bodies cannot exist in a spiritual realm. A spiritual body is needed. This is given to us as a resurrected body.

Before discussing the resurrected body, we need to pause to consider our physical bodies, our *sarx*. For earthly life the physical body is indispensable. How well we live and how long we live on earth depends largely on the care we take of our bodies.

Inherently the Christian regards the body as good. God created it, and everything he created is good. "And God saw everything that he had made, and behold, it was very good" (Genesis 1:31). Christians do not agree with the Greek philosophers, Gnostics, and Manichaeans that all matter, including the human body, is evil. Anything material is in itself bad, they say. To them only the spirit is pure and good. In contrast, Christians hold their bodies in great respect. The body is the crown of God's creation: we are fearfully and wonderfully made. There is no organ, drive, instinct, or function of the body that is sinful. There is no need to be ashamed of any part or function of the body. It is our abuse and misuse of the body that is evil. When we abuse the body with excessive alcohol, tobacco, drugs, and illicit sex, we are sinning.

Nevertheless, the physical body is mortal and is scheduled to die. Death is a normal event in all nature. God never intended human beings to live physically forever. The physical body was made for this world only. The day will come for each of us when a minister will say at the committal, "earth to earth, ashes to ashes, and dust to dust."

In spite of this, the physical body can be used by God on earth. The body is the temple of the Holy Spirit (1 Corinthians 6:19). God the Spirit chooses to dwell within us. Since the body is the house of God, we need to treat it with reverence. If the Holy Spirit dwells in our bodies, our responsibility is to see that the vessel is holy. Our bodies also can be offered to God as living sacrifices. What we do with our bodies can honor and glorify God. "Whatever you do in word or deed, do all to the glory of God." In Philippians Paul expresses the hope that Christ will be honored in his body, "whether by life or death" (1:20).

The Resurrected Body

Now we are ready to ask, "With what kind of body do they come?" (1 Corinthians 15:35). The resurrected body is a body in terms of *soma*, the total person of body, mind, and soul. The Bible is emphatic that people in heaven are *not* disembodied spirits. At this point we are in total disagreement with the Greeks and Gnostics and all others who hold strictly to a bodiless afterlife.

There are people who hold to the view that the resurrected body is a literal physical body, identical to the body we have on earth. Paul had to face this problem and he flatly said, "Flesh and blood cannot inherit the kingdom of God" (1 Corinthians 15:50).

Because heaven is not a physical place with physical bodies, Pope John Paul II assured his people some years ago that, while man and woman retain their sense of sexuality, there will be no marriage or sex in heaven. Jesus also said that in heaven there is no marriage.

How literal we can become was shown in a letter to Ann Landers a few years ago. A woman wrote to Ann: "I have six large gold crowns in my mouth and I know they are worth a lot of money. I firmly believe that there will be a resurrection, and it will come sooner than most people think. If I leave the gold crowns to a relative, I would then have to have the crowns replaced after I am resurrected. Dentistry may be a lot more expensive by the time I rise again." A few weeks later someone answered the letter concerning the gold crowns. The answer was that the resurrection will transform the body to perfection. In that case, the first woman would not have to be concerned with her crowns, for her teeth would be filled and flawless.

In 1 Corinthians 15, Paul gives his most thorough and detailed discussion of the resurrected body. He says there is a body for every specific need. Thus, for the spiritual world we are given a spiritual

214

body. The perishable physical body becomes imperishable; the physical becomes spiritual; the mortal becomes immortal. The natural becomes supernatural. The weak becomes powerful. The corruptible body becomes incorruptible. In other words, the spiritual body does not die.

When we physically die, we shall all be changed "in a moment, in the twinkling of an eye...." We shall be given a spiritual body which will enable us to live in the spiritual world where Christ and the saints live.

Implications

What does this resurrected body have to do with us? Does it make any difference what kind of body we will have in the afterlife? Indeed, it does make a difference how we regard our present bodies and what we do with them. The Bible teaches that Christians at death will be given a spiritual body for a spiritual life with God. This knowledge has implications for our lives now and in the future.

Identification

The first implication is that having a body enables a person to maintain his/her identity. Each person is a handmade individual for earth and heaven. Christians, therefore, repudiate the false idea of reincarnation which teaches that a person returns to earth after death for another life as another person, maybe even as an animal or insect. The scriptures insist that each person has but one life. It came from God to live on earth for a divine purpose and will return to God in heaven by faith in Christ.

When a person dies, he/she is not like a drop of rainwater that falls into a lake and loses its identity. The drop of water that falls into a lake does not cease to exist but loses its identity. Once it has fallen into the lake, who can separate it as that drop of water? We are not like drops of water falling at death into the ocean of God's humanity. Each of us is a person in his/her own right for all eternity. When King Saul went to a fortune teller to speak to the dead prophet, Samuel responded, "Why have you disturbed me by bringing me up?" (1 Samuel 28:15). At the Transfiguration Moses and

Elijah, dead for centuries, appeared as individuals to Jesus. Each person has infinite importance to God. He knows the name of each person. "Behold, I have graven you on the palms of my hands" (Isaiah 49:16). And that name on God's hands is ineradicable and indelible.

Fellowship

Because in heaven we have bodies, we not only retain our identities but we can know each other and have fellowship with each other. Often the bereaved ask, "Will we know our loved ones in heaven?" Indeed, we will recognize each other because our resurrection bodies will be akin to our earthly ones. Our resurrected bodies will be similar to Jesus' resurrected body. To prove that he was the same person who suffered and died, he showed them the nail prints in his hands and feet. Yet he had a glorified body which was spiritual to enable him to enter and leave closed rooms and to appear or disappear at will. In Jesus' parable of Dives and Lazarus, Dives saw Abraham and asked him to send Lazarus to cool his tongue with a drop of water. Apparently Jesus thought that in the afterlife people would know each other and would communicate with each other. In 1 Corinthians 13 Paul says, "Now I know in part; then I shall understand fully, even as I have been fully understood." Now we see in part, but later we shall know each other and Christ "face to face." Moreover, the church is defined as "the communion of saints," a fellowship of believers. What is true of the visible and militant church on earth is even more true for the invisible and triumphant church in heaven. This fellowship is possible because we are bodies and not pure spirits, and through these bodies we can have fellowship and can communicate with each other.

Funerals

What shall we do with the dead physical body? If we believe we will need it in heaven, we will do all we can to preserve it for the next life. Today many are trying to preserve the physical body through expensive funerals. We embalm the body to preserve it, just as the Egyptians did in ancient times. We may buy expensive caskets of copper with glass coverings to protect the dead body from the earth. Many place expensive caskets in waterproof vaults. To make the corpse comfortable (!) we have luxurious mattresses and silk linings for the interior of the caskets. To make the dead look as though they are sleeping in comfort, we use cosmetics to give the appearance of health.

This physical body has served its purpose on earth. It is no longer needed in a spiritual world. God has replaced it with a better, immortal body of the spirit. It is downright foolish to try to preserve something that God intended to return to the earth: "ashes to ashes." Out of the dust humanity was created and to dust it is to return. Why do we not accept the reality of death instead of making believe that this physical body is going to be resuscitated for eternal life? It is a waste of money which could be better spent on the living who are in need.

Cremation

As the population grows in America, there is less land for cemeteries. Moreover, the average funeral has become for many too expensive: grave, monument, embalming, casket, and funeral home charges. Cremation, therefore, is growing in popularity.

Cremation is disturbing to some people. The question is whether a body should be allowed to deteriorate normally or whether the process should be hastened by burning. The thought of burning up a loved one is repulsive to some people. The question is whether a Christian can in good conscience cremate a loved one. In addition, cremation removes the possibility of honoring the dead by caring for the lot, visiting the grave, and placing flowers on the grave. Cremation seems to give the impression that the deceased by cremation is annihilated. There is a difference between having the body brought into the church in a casket covered with a beautiful pall in contrast to a memorial service with or without a box of ashes.

If the physical body will not exist in the next life, there is no need to try to preserve it as long as we can. Again, we see that the physical body was intended by God to return to the earth. Moreover, the resurrected body is not the physical one, but a new spiritual body which is incorruptible and immortal. Since the physical body is destined to become ashes, it does not matter whether it is sooner or later. It is merely a matter of time. Thus, it becomes a matter of personal choice and taste. It is really not a moral or spiritual issue. No doubt, God would look with favor on either cremation or the traditional burial in the ground. Local and personal circumstances would probably decide the method of disposing of a body which has fulfilled its purpose on earth.

Organ Donations

The question is often raised whether one should upon death give organs to needy people that they might continue to live. Today in America there are needed as replacement organs 30,000 kidneys, 75,000 hearts, 5,000 livers, and 10,000 pancreases. Yet each year 2,400 died for lack of a donated organ.

How should a Christian feel about giving an organ at death in order for another person to live? Since we know that we will not need this body in the next life and since we know that the body with all its organs will decay, it seems sensible that we should offer our organs if they are in good condition. Not to do so may seem selfish and uncaring. Some time ago I was in a discussion group where there was a man in his forties who had a heart transplant. He was now using the heart of a youth in his twenties, a youth killed in an auto accident. Without the donation, that man would be dead, too. Can anyone give another person a more precious gift than an organ which enabled that person to live?

The Resurrection Of The Body

According to the Apostles' Creed, Christians believe in the "resurrection of the body." This raises the question in some minds whether there is a resurrection and what is resurrected if there is a resurrection. What are we saying and what do we mean when each Sunday we confess that we believe in "the resurrection of the body?"

Is There A Resurrection?

Which of the following is your position? Check your stand.

1. ___ I do not believe the physical body comes back to life.
2. ___ I do not believe in a resurrection, because my life will continue in my children.
3. ___ I do not believe the body is resurrected, because the physical body is inherently evil.
4. ___ I believe the resurrection has taken place, because I was born again at my baptism.
5. ___ I believe in a final resurrection, because Jesus rose from the dead.
6. ___ I believe in a resurrection of the dead, because Jesus believed in it.

When Is The Resurrection?

When do you think the resurrection takes place? Check your opinion.

1. ___ When a Christian dies and goes to live with Christ.
2. ___ When a nonbeliever dies and goes to Sheol (Hades).
3. ___ When Christ returns to judge the nations.
4. ___ When a person accepts Jesus as Lord and Savior.

Why The Resurrection?

Fill in the blanks by reading the biblical references to get the answer, "why?"

1. To give every person an opportunity to give an _____ of his/her life. Read Romans 14:12.
2. To enable believers to have _____. Read Philippians 1:21.
3. To _____ the nations. Read Matthew 25:32.
4. To _____ the faithful. Read 2 Timothy 4:8.
5. To _____ the wicked. Read Matthew 25:41-46.

Is The Physical Body Resurrected?

Which of the following are true or false? Circle your answer.

T F 1. There is no place for a physical body in a spiritual realm.

T F 2. It is natural for a physical body to die.

T F 3. The physical body houses the soul on earth.

T F 4. The physical body is the temple of the Holy Spirit.

T F 5. It is a sin to waste, harm, or destroy the human body.

T F 6. An attempt to preserve the dead physical body is foolish.

T F 7. Cremation is an acceptable way for Christians to permit the body to come to "ashes to ashes."

T F 8. Since at death one no longer needs the physical body, it is charitable to donate one's organs that others may live.

Is The Spiritual Body Resurrected?

According to Paul, God will give us a new body to live with Christ in heaven. What kind of a body is it? To get the answers to the following questions read 1 Corinthians 15:35-54 and 2 Corinthians 5:1-10.

1. What kind of a body do we need for life after death?

2. Can a physical body exist in a spiritual world?

3. What are the characteristics of the resurrected body?

4. Where and when are we given this new body?

5. Will we know each other in heaven?

6. Does one lose one's identity after death?

7. Will we be able to communicate with each other in heaven?

Chapter 17

The Life Everlasting

"If a man die, shall he live again?" (Job 14:14). From the beginning of the human race, humanity has been asking Job's question. Through the ages, people have given different answers. Some say "man" will live again. Some say he will not. Others do not know. In a mighty crescendo the Apostles' Creed ends "and the life everlasting." That seems to be it; what more can be said? Yet questions come to mind. Does "everlasting life" mean that the human body dies but the soul continues to live forever? Or does the phrase mean that we Christians believe that we shall never die? Does it mean that we must die before everlasting life begins?

What Are We Talking About?

This talk about life after death can be confusing. We may use terms that we do not understand or we may get them mixed up. Is immortality the same as eternal life? Is there any difference between eternal life and everlasting life? We need to define our terms.

Immortality is not the same as eternal life. It is an ancient Greek teaching that the soul at death drops the body and continues its existence forever. The soul is like a spark that flies up to join the cosmic fire. The soul loses its identity in the oversoul. According to this view, immortality is a natural endowment of the soul.

Everlasting and eternal mean the same. The New Testament usually speaks of "eternal life." It is a life of quality because it is the very life of God. This divine life is primarily a life of quality which endures forever and can therefore be described as "everlasting." Life is everlasting when the life is in Christ.

Two Kinds Of Life

The Greeks had two words for "life" and both appear in the New Testament. One is *bios* from which we get "biology." It refers

223

to biological and physical life. It is not true life but mere existence. This is life in terms of quantity and extension. Methuselah, the oldest man in the Bible, had this kind of life. He lived 969 years, but there is no record of any contribution he made to the welfare of society.

The other Greek word is *zoe*. It is used to denote true life, the quality of life. It is spiritual life with God as the source of life. While *bios* is temporal, *zoe* is eternal. The one deals with the body and the other with the soul. But this eternal life also has quantity, for it extends through eternity. To distinguish this type of life from the former, the New Testament uses "eternal life."

Two Kinds Of Death

As there are two kinds of life, there are two kinds of death. The *bios* type of life ends in physical death. The body declines, deteriorates, and dies. This is in accord with the natural order, for all living things die, including *Homo sapiens*. If a human were only a physical body, the person would come to an end. In this case, death has the last word and is the ultimate victor over life.

There is another kind of death. The Bible speaks of death in terms of separation from God. "The soul that sins shall die" (Ezekiel 18:4). Sin is the dreadful agent that separates us from God. To be apart from God, from life, love, joy, and peace, is to be dead. Does this mean that the soul is exterminated or extinguished? If so, there would be a merciful nothingness. However, the Bible teaches that a soul apart from God, living in death, is in hell, a state of misery. Paul describes the condition in hell: "They shall suffer the punishment of eternal destruction and exclusion from the presence of the Lord and from the glory of his might" (2 Thessalonians 1:9). As there is eternal life, there is also everlasting death. It is to save us from this fate that God gave his Son to die for us and to reinstate us with God in whom we have eternal life. The scriptures repeatedly assure us that God does not want a single soul to perish or to be lost or to go to hell. In Christ, God the Father gave his very self to prevent people from going to everlasting death.

Can You Prove It?

If you say in the Apostles' Creed that you believe in "the life everlasting," can you prove it? How could anyone prove its reality? No one has come back from death to tell us all about it. It becomes ultimately a matter of faith. That is why the phrase is part of the creed which says, "I believe." What do you believe? You believe in the life everlasting.

Nonbelievers

Not everyone has faith in the existence of life after death. There are people who prefer not to believe in it. In 1990 a Gallup poll indicated that 23 percent of Americans do not believe in life after death.

It may be to our advantage if there is no everlasting life. If there is no future life, then this life is the end of all things. We will not have to face God's judgment. We will not be called upon to give an account of our lives.

Moreover, if there is no future life, we do not have to fear any punishment for our sins. If there is no future life, there is no hell! We will not have to fear death because there will be no punishment for our sins. Death can be an easy way out of a life lived in selfishness, crime, and destruction. You can then do your worst and by death flee from all retribution.

Again, if there is no life after death, we can live this life in a carefree manner. We can say, "You only live once! You had better make the most of life now. There is no tomorrow. When you are dead, you are dead all over and forever." This would make us 100 percent materialistic. Why would we care about character or the quality of life? Why not live it up, get out of it all you can, walk over people for your own gain, and get while the getting's good? Paul says that if the dead are not raised, we may say, "Let us eat and drink, for tomorrow we die" (1 Corinthians 15:32).

Believers

For Christians the position of the unbelievers is not for them. If one-fourth do not believe in life after death, three-fourths do. For most of us, death is not the final word. Something in us says there is something more. Is it an instinct like that of a homing pigeon that always brings the bird home? Is it like a compass always turning to the north pole? Or could it be like the urge for self-preservation? We want to live. We long for life. This longing for immortality has existed from the beginning of the human race. In primitive religions there are paintings, practices, and stories of life after death. Indeed, no one can prove it. It is a matter of faith. Jesus did not try to prove it. He simply assumed there was life everlasting and he showed how we can live forever. When he told Martha at the time her brother Lazarus died that he was "the resurrection and the life," he asked her, "Do you believe this?"

Though life everlasting cannot be proved, Christians have good reasons for believing it to be a reality. For one thing, we believe in the future life because of the very nature of God. The Bible reveals God as Spirit. He is God the Holy Spirit, the author and creator of life. In the Old Testament the word for "life" is "breath." When Adam was created, God breathed into him and he became a living soul. He had God the Spirit in him bearing the image of God. The Hebrew word for "spirit" is "breath." God the Spirit gives life to a person who is born of the Spirit and therefore has God's life within. Paul teaches, "He who sows to the Spirit will from the Spirit reap eternal life" (Galatians 6:8). Again he writes, "The written code kills, but the Spirit gives life" (2 Corinthians 3:6). The life given by the Spirit code never ends, because the Spirit is God who cannot die. God therefore is life. When we have God in us through the Holy Spirit we have everlasting life. Jesus said God is not the God of the dead but of the living.

Another good reason for believing in life after death is the resurrection of Jesus. If he did not rise, as Saint Paul says, we also will not rise to eternal life. Without the resurrection our faith is in vain. We are still in our sins and death is permanent. Jesus' resurrection is our proof that there is life after death. God raised him and brought him out of the tomb on Easter. His rising assures us that life is stronger than death. Consequently death has been conquered. Since this is true, we can see how vital and essential Jesus' resurrection is to our faith in eternal life. Without the resurrection, we would still be asking, "If a man dies, will he live again?" For this reason the resurrection is the keystone in the arch of the Christian religion. Because we believe in the resurrection, we believe in everlasting life. And why do we believe in the resurrection? Because Christ lives in our hearts.

A third reason for our faith in life after death is in the nature of humanity. Who is "man"? Is humanity nothing more than any other part of creation or are people different? The Bible tells us that a human being is a special creature, the crown and glory of creation. Because of being made in the image of God, a human has inherent dignity and worth. This worth is based on the fact that a human is both a creature of God by creation and a child by redemption. Above the rest of creation, a person is a "living soul" akin to God. If a person were only a material thing, he/she could be expected to die. But God did not make humans to die. He made people to live and to have someone to love. If people died, God would be defeating his own purpose. Who then would he have to love?

Add to these reasons for believing in life after death the fact of the promises of God. God has promised us eternal life. Jesus said, "In my Father's house there are many mansions ... I go to prepare a place for you" (John 14:2, 3). Listen to his promise: "He who believes in me, though he die, yet shall he live" (John 11:25). It is a fact that God has never broken his promises and he never will. He is God, a God who is faithful and who can be trusted to do what he says.

What Is The Life Everlasting?

For many of us the subject of eternal life is a mystery. We do not have the faintest idea of what it is or how it is received. The scriptures give us answers. Consider some of them.

Eternal Life Is A Gift

There is no earning life after death because of our character or accomplishments. Of course, it cannot be bought, because life is beyond price. No one has enough money to extend one's life for a single hour. Yet some keep searching for immortality.

"The life everlasting" is a divine gift and not a human achievement. Only God can give life that never ends, because he is life. In his first letter, John explains, "And this is the testimony, that God *gave* us eternal life, and this life is in his Son" (1 John 5:11). Eternal life then is not a native endowment but something given to us by God. We will not live forever because we are human beings. Unless we have God in us, we will spend eternity in death. To have God is to have life forever.

Eternal Life Is Life In Christ

Eternal life is having Christ in you. "He who has the Son has life" (1 John 5:12). Life everlasting is identified with Christ and his resurrection. It needs to be remembered that, until Christ came, there was little to no assurance of life everlasting. Sheol (Hades) was the place of the dead, located under the earth, a place of darkness and gloom. There was no exit in Sheol. There are only a few glimpses of life eternal in the Old Testament (Psalm 49:15; 73:23; Isaiah 26:19).

Having eternal life depends upon our having Christ. To have Christ calls for knowing him. "And this is eternal life, that they know thee the only true God, and Jesus Christ whom thou hast sent" (John 17:3). To know Jesus is to have more than a knowledge of him. It is to have a personal relationship with him made possible by faith. To have Christ in order to have eternal life means to believe in Christ. He comes to us and in us by faith. When Jesus tells Martha that he is the resurrection and the life, he asks her, "Do you believe this?" John tells us that God so loved the world that he gave his Son that whoever *believes* in him might have everlasting life (John 3:16). Furthermore, to have Christ and his life means discipleship. When the rich young ruler asked Jesus what he had to do to inherit eternal life, Jesus told him to sell all and follow him. To serve Christ, to be his disciple, to give your life in his service is to have eternal life.

Eternal Life Is A Present Possession

The common view is that life everlasting begins at death. Most of us want to go to heaven, but we do not want to die to get there! It is a falsehood to believe that one must first die to have eternal life. This life begins here and now from the time that Christ is accepted by faith. When Dietrich Bonhoeffer was taken from his Nazi cell for execution, he said to one of the prisoners, "This is the end, but for me the beginning of life." According to the New Testament, that was not true. Eternal life did not begin at the time of his execution. John was writing to living people when he said, "I write this to you who believe in the name of the Son of God, that you may know that you have eternal life" (1 John 5:13). To the repentant thief on the cross, Jesus assured him, "Today you will be with me in paradise" (Luke 23:43). In other words, if we do not have eternal life now before we die, we will not have it after death. Now we have life eternal in Christ, and we are assured that nothing — no person, no power, no creature — can ever separate us from this life in Christ (Romans 8:38).

Eternal Life Depends On Faith

Now we have seen that life everlasting is in possessing the Spirit of God and in having Christ in us. But how does that happen? How can we get this life eternal? Since it is a gift of God, it is something that needs to be received. How then do we get this life in us as a personal possession?

Faith is the receptive agent. It is the hand that takes the gift that God offers. By faith we believe God will give us this gift. By faith we reach out to take the gift and make it our very own. By faith Christ lives in us, and as long as he is in us, we have eternal life. That means that faith is indispensable to living forever with God in heaven. Moreover, faith enables us to keep that life. Lose faith and Christ is rejected. Not to have Christ is not to have life. It is a lifetime challenge for us to keep the faith in order to possess eternal life.

What Difference Does It Make?

What does faith in "the life everlasting" mean to us living today? If there is life after death, we know what it means to people after death. But what difference does this faith make to us here and now?

Fear Of Death Removed

We naturally fear death because we are afraid of the unknown. Every person must come to terms with death and hopefully face it with confidence and courage. Many feel like the short story writer O. Henry. When dying, he said to his nurse, "Nurse, bring me a candle." "A candle?" she asked. "Why do you want a candle?" "Because," he grimly answered, "I'm afraid to go home in the dark."

If we have faith in Christ and in his resurrection, if we have faith in the promises of God, and if eternal life is a present possession, the fear of death is removed. Then we will look at death as an opportunity to be more fully in and with Christ. And to be with Christ is to have everything good: life, love, peace, and joy. With Johann Sebastian Bach we can sing, "Come, sweet death, come, holy rest."

Comfort For The Bereaved

It is not only a matter of concern for our death but, when dear ones die ahead of us, how shall we be comforted? Who or what can dry our tears and heal our broken hearts? It is the assurance of life eternal that brings us comfort. We are comforted that our loved one died in Christ. Because of this, our loved one is with Christ in all joy and peace.

Because of our faith in Christ, we never see our loved ones for the last time. There will be a reunion of family and friends. We shall recognize, know, and communicate with each other. Our fellowship will be in our common devotion to Christ. Death is but a temporary loss of loved ones for the permanent gain of life together forever.

Hope For The Future

Believing in "the life everlasting" gives us reason to hope for the future. This life is not all there is. There is a new and better life ahead. Some day justice will be done and faithfulness will be rewarded. Truth will out! Love will win! Righteousness will prevail! We live today in this hope.

Our faces are not to the setting sun but to the rising sun. Near the end of his life, General William Booth, founder of the Salvation

Army, became blind. One day he and his daughter, Evangeline, faced the setting sun in all its glory. She begged her father to look and asked if he did not see at least a gleam of its beauty. Quietly and confidently he replied, "I cannot see the sun set but I shall see it rise!"

How Important Is The Church?

As we draw to a close our study on the third article of the Apostles' Creed, we ask, "How important is the church?" According to the Apostles' Creed, the church is the product of God the Holy Spirit. He created the church by making and gathering believers. Why did God the Spirit create the church as the fellowship of believers? Why was he not content to make individual Christians who would go their solitary way? The Spirit created the church to reconcile the world to God. To the church was given the Word and sacraments, the marks of the true church. Through these means of grace people received "the forgiveness of sins, the resurrection of the body, and the life everlasting." These three add up to salvation, getting right with God. A saved person is one who has been forgiven, who will receive a spiritual body at death, and life that will never end in heaven.

Because of this truth, the church has claimed, throughout her history, that outside the church there is no salvation. If the Word and sacraments bring grace to believers, it is a reasonable conclusion that belonging to the church is necessary for salvation. The church consists of God's saved people: called, chosen, redeemed, and strengthened by the Spirit. In the third century, Saint Cyprian claimed, *"Extra ecclesiam nulla salus"* — "Outside the church no salvation." This truth was repeated in the Westminster Confession of Faith: "The visible church is the kingdom of the Lord Jesus Christ, the house and family of God, out of which there is no ordinary possibility of salvation."

Martin Luther held the same position. He wrote, "I believe that no one can be saved who is not in this gathering or community [church], harmoniously sharing the same faith with it, the same Word, sacraments, hope, and love." Again he wrote: "I believe there is forgiveness of sin nowhere else than in this community [church],

231

and that beyond it, nothing can help to gain it — no good deeds, no matter how many, or how great they may be."

If there is no salvation outside the church, come into her and be saved! If you are in the church, stay in her to remain saved. For the salvation of the world love, support, serve, and extend your church.

A Summary Of The Third Article Of The Apostles' Creed

This You Can Believe

I believe that I cannot by my own reason or strength believe in Jesus Christ my Lord, or come to him; but the Holy Ghost has called me through the gospel, enlightened me with his gifts, and sanctified and preserved me in the true faith, in like manner as he calls, gathers, enlightens, and sanctifies the whole Christian church on earth, and preserves it in union with Jesus Christ in the true faith; in which Christian church he daily forgives all my sins, and the sins of all believers, and will raise up me and all the dead at the last day, and will grant everlasting life to me and to all who believe in Christ. This is most certainly true.

— Martin Luther, *The Small Catechism*

The Life Everlasting

Two Kinds

There are two kinds of life. Which kind is "life everlasting"? Below are listed the characteristics of both kinds. After a review of the marks of each kind, label the lists "Physical" and "Spiritual."

_____ Life	_____ Life
1. Life on earth	1. Life in heaven
2. Quantity of life	2. Quality of life
3. Natural possession	3. Divine gift
4. Limited	4. Unlimited

Likewise there are two kinds of death. Fill in the blanks according to "Physical" and "Spiritual." Which is which?

_____ Death	_____ Death
1. End of life on earth	1. End of life in God
2. Normal	2. Separation from God
3. Natural	3. Existence in hell
4. Nothingness	4. Rejection of God

Life After Death

According to a 1990 Gallup poll, 23 percent of the American people say they do not believe there is life after death. What do you think of some of their reasons for not believing? Is it better not to believe than to believe? React to these contentions:

1. If there is no life after death, one does not have to give an account of one's life on earth.

2. If there is no life after death, there is no divine judgment with fear of hell.

3. If there is no life after death, death means the end of a life of misery and trouble. This is good news for those who say with Job, "I loathe my life" (Job 7:16).

4. If there is no life after death, we can eat, drink, and be merry, for life will soon be over.

On the other hand, Christians believe in "the life everlasting." Why do they? Can they prove that life continues after physical death? What is the basis of this faith? What do you think of these arguments?

1. God is life and the God only of the living, not of the dead.

2. Jesus' resurrection assures us of life beyond the grave.

3. Eternal life is a gift to believers in Christ.

4. The gift of eternal life is accepted by faith.

5. God's promise of eternal life can be trusted.

6. Eternal life begins with faith in Christ here and now and is a personal existence.

7. Your additional reason: _____

The Difference

What difference does it make in our lives to say that we believe in "the life everlasting"? Think about it and list the difference you think such faith makes:

1. In respect to death _____

2. In respect to bereavement _____

3. In respect to hope for the future _____

A Service Of Faith Renewal

Dear Friends in Christ: At an earlier time in our lives, we were received by grace into God's Kingdom through Holy Baptism. Since that event, we have come to a better understanding of our faith. We are here to re-confess our faith in Christ and in our triune God. I, therefore, call upon each of us, in the presence of God and these witnesses, to reaffirm our faith by answering the following questions:

Do you renounce the devil and all his works and all his ways?
People: Yes, I renounce them.

Do you believe in God the Father Almighty, creator of heaven and earth?
People: Yes, I believe in God the Father Almighty, creator of heaven and earth.

Do you believe in Jesus Christ as your Lord and Savior?
People: Yes, I believe in Jesus Christ, his only Son, our Lord. He was conceived by the Holy Spirit, born of the virgin Mary. He suffered under Pontius Pilate, was crucified, died, and was buried. He descended to the dead. On the third day he rose again. He ascended into heaven, and is seated at the right hand of God the Father almighty. He will come again to judge the living and the dead.

Do you believe in the Holy Spirit, your guide and comforter?
People: Yes, I believe in the Holy Spirit; the holy catholic church, the communion of saints; the forgiveness of sins; the resurrection of the body; and the life everlasting.

Do you promise to continue in this faith and in the vows of your baptism?
People: Yes, I promise.

Do you promise to pray daily, to read the Bible regularly, and to receive the Holy Communion faithfully?
People: Yes, by the help of God.

The Lord be with you.
People: And also with you.

Let us pray.

Almighty and most merciful God, we thank you for this opportunity to renew our love, faith, and loyalty to you. We pray that we may ever remain true to you, that no love of the world may lead us away from you, but that in joyful obedience we may ever know you more perfectly, love you more fervently, and serve you more effectively in word and deed. Grant, dear Lord, that we may always be a blessing to our fellow men, a glory to you and faithful disciples of Jesus Christ, your Son, in whose name we pray:
People: Our Father, who art in heaven....

The peace of God which passes all understanding, keep your hearts and minds through Christ Jesus.
People: Amen

All joining hands may sing or say:

We Believe In One True God
Tobias Clausnitzer
Trans. by Catherine Winkworth
RATISBON 77.77.77

We believe in one true God,
Father, Son, and Holy Ghost,
everpresent help in need,
praised by all the heavenly host;
by whose mighty power alone
all is made and wrought and done.

We believe in Jesus Christ,
Son of God and Mary's Son,
who descended from his throne
and for us salvation won;
by whose cross and death are we
rescued from sin's misery.

We confess the Holy Ghost,
who from both fore'er proceeds;
who upholds and comforts us
in all trials, fears, and needs.
Blest and Holy Trinity,
praise forever be to thee!